LOREDANA MEDURI & ALESSANDRO SPANU

TH
FISHER
WISDOM

A story about happiness and trusting the magic of beginnings

BE MORE Publishing
First published in Germany by Meduri-Spanu GbR 2021

Loredana Meduri and Alessandro Spanu assert the moral right to be identified as the authors of this work.

ISBN 978-3-98-257274-1

AN UNEXPECTED ENCOUNTER AT THE PIER

__________"Hello, did you sleep well? Can I make you a coffee? Would you like to have breakfast?"

The woman with thick black hair smiled kindly at me from behind the reception desk. She must have been in her forties. She was slender but had curves in all the right places. Her large dark eyes shone awake and alert.

I, on the other hand, had a headache because I had not been able to keep my eyes shut the night before. Too many things about work were running through my head. Normally, I was able to switch off well when I was on vacation, but this time it was different. Even the journey here was long: the flight was quite turbulent, and the queue at the rental car counter was endless. This is not how I had imagined my first day off.

It was half past six. My plan for the day was to run twelve or fifteen kilometres, but my right knee, which lately had been aching more and more, had persuaded me to take it easy. My doctor had recommended surgery, but something in me resisted it.

"Good morning," I said to the lady who was still looking at me with a very friendly smile. "Thank you, but I didn't order breakfast," I continued.
"It is included in the price", replied the lady encouragingly. "I'd be happy to prepare something for you".
"Ok, in that case, I'll have a cappuccino, thank you".
I still didn't quite understand how I found that place. It was all very simple, but clean, and it reassured me. I usually only looked for luxury hotels, never really for holiday apartments. This house, however, I don't know why, had enticed me.
My apartment was part of a complex of five or six older individual houses. The guests were completely independent. They gave you keys to access a whole floor of one of the houses and if you needed anything, you went to reception.
"Please take a seat. I'll bring you a cappuccino right away".
"Oh, and I'd also like to have a map of the area. Do you have one?" I asked.
„Of course. I'll bring it to you right away."
I went out onto the terrace. It appeared as though I was the only guest. Maybe everyone else was still asleep. I couldn't help but think of Anna. She also didn't like getting up early when she was on vacation.
When she had kissed me goodbye, I had read in her eyes, as always, that she would have liked to accompa-

ny me here. But I desperately needed time to myself. We had already discussed this several times. One week in late spring and one in autumn: those were "Andrew's times". In summer and winter, I always went on a week-long trip with her. It seemed like a good solution to me.

Without these short breaks just for me, I would have gone crazy. There was too much hustle in the bank: too much stress, constant changes to react to, customer demands... I was in charge of the large commercial customers, who always had to deal with millions.

Where there is a lot of money, there is also a lot of pressure and the high demands from all sides. It was not uncommon for our board members to take all the pressure they were under out on us.

A few years earlier, another Swiss company, which provided financial services, would have liked to take me on board with them. They had heard about me and my successes. For a few days, I imagined what it would be like to move to the Alps, with fantastic ski slopes right nearby... But in the end I refused. I felt comfortable in the bank where I was working, even though there was some friction with the members of the board of directors, whom I would have gladly catapulted to the other side of the planet, one by one, on a regular basis. At least, I was earning well, even if, jokingly, I called my earnings a sort of compensation for damages.

The lady brought me the cappuccino. She also brought a plate with a warm, fragrant croissant. Before I could refuse it, as I was actively trying to avoid the combination of white flour and fat as much as possible, she said to me: “You must taste the croissant! My mother makes them with her own hands. It is filled with apricot jam. And here is your map.” She handed me a very basic map and a small map of the place, in which the house where we were was marked by hand.
“Thank you.”
“Enjoy your meal. If you need me, call!” With these words, the lady disappeared towards the reception. Looking over her shoulder, I noticed that she was dressed in black from head to toe. Her flat shoes and her thin stockings were also black. Why wasn‘t she wearing something a little brighter or floral?
In front of the house there was a large garden with olive trees and oleanders. From here, the sea was a thin strip of blue beyond the neighbouring houses, even though the internet ad promised a sea view. The sea could probably be seen from one of the other houses where I didn‘t live. “What the heck,” I thought. “Anything to make money!”
As an alternative to Abruzzo, I had thought of doing a bike ride around Lake Garda or going trekking for a week in Nepal. But there was too little time for Nepal and in the autumn I was already planning to cross the

Alps by bike. So, for this year's spring, I had chosen the sea.

Anna also thought it was a good idea, but I was there without her. I knew I hurt her. But Lake Garda would have hurt her the same. Everything would have hurt her. It didn't matter where I went.

To be honest, I couldn't understand why she didn't make use of the time that I was away to do something for herself or to do something with her friends. Since we didn't have any children, we were free and independent. But Anna always stayed at home and overwhelmed herself with work. She worked in the accounting department of a large automobile company.

The cappuccino was good, much better than the one from the vending machine at the office. Even the croissant upheld the expectation. As I chewed, I thought about how full my inbox was. Oh well! My replacement would take care of it in my absence. I had already left. It was in that moment that I realised that, apart from the chirping of some birds and a moped in the distance, I wasn't hearing anything. There was no plane in the sky and not a single cloud. Right after breakfast, I decided to go to the beach for a walk. If my knee stopped acting up, I could always go for a jog around noon. When I got up and walked back towards the reception, the lady smiled at me again. Maybe she was the owner? I couldn't tell.

"Have a nice day!" she said.
I nodded. "You too, thank you."
"If you wish to go down to the sea, it's not far away," she added.
"Keep walking on the road, this side. After about two hundred meters, a small alley on the right leads through the houses. Then there are only bushes, among which a path opens. You will find it."
"Well, I'll make my way through the bushes then," I said, smiling.
"You will like the coast, trust me!." I could still hear her voice, but I was already in the sun outside the building. I found the path through the bushes that the lady had told me about and followed it. From outside no one could have seen me due to how thick the vegetation was. I didn't meet a soul when I resurfaced in the sun, on the other side of the bushes. Before me, the sea stretched to the horizon. A dreamlike view, like in the catalog of a major tour operator. I breathed deeply. Being by the sea gave me an indescribable feeling of freedom that I often missed at home. Anna and I were well-off, but that large apartment, two cars and all the insurance policies had to be paid for. We also didn't want to limit ourselves in food and clothes. It was what it was.
Behind the walkway, the path descended steeply to the beach. There were no stairs, so I had to walk some

more. To my left, a long jetty plunged into the sea. At its end was a simple log cabin. Beyond the hut I could see large rectangular nets attached to the jetty with long struts and ropes. They looked like huge cobwebs. Everything looked strangely bare and fragile. Weren‘t the fishing nets supposed to be offshore? That way of arranging them was strange. I pulled up to the dock to take a closer look. It did not give me a sense of being particularly stable, even though the bottom rested on large poles, and steel cables further strengthened the entire construction. The whole structure swayed quite a bit. Or was it just my impression because the sea was moving so much?

"Okay," I thought. "Now you‘ve seen it too: a seaside hut with nets hanging from a pier". The cabin seemed uninhabited. There was not a living soul in sight. I was continuing to start my walk when I noticed a blackboard. It was fixed next to a doorpost made of old wooden beams, hung up at eye level. A sentence had been scribbled on the blackboard with chalk. "What would you do if you weren‘t afraid?"

I reread it. Some kind of philosopher must have lived in there. In a way, the question irritated me. For the first time I felt like my professor must have felt, when, after we drew all over the blackboard during recess, he returned to the classroom, took the sponge and erased everything, flustered.

I too felt the need to delete that question. Suddenly someone appeared next to the hut. He was an elderly gentleman, with shoulder-length gray hair, a pale polo shirt, baggy gray trousers, and a windbreaker.
He greeted me and came towards me.
"Good morning! Come in." He said.
To tell the truth, I didn't really want to set foot on that rickety walkway.
"Come in!" he said again. By now he was so close that I could see the brilliant blue of his irises and the many wrinkles that lined his face. "Like a fishing net", I thought. The man looked like a fisherman.
"Thanks, I just wanted to take a look."
I wanted to leave quickly, but he continued: "I'm glad you're here. I was waiting for you!" This was starting to creep me out. Part of me wanted to leave as fast as possible. The other part - the one who loved adventures and who would take off on a mountain bike down very steep mountains on holiday - wanted to stay. I was torn.
The man was barefoot. We were now facing each other. He on one side of the door frame, I on the other. He seemed very well groomed and he smiled at me as if we knew each other. „What's your name?"
"Andrew", I replied.
"Andrew", he repeated. "Welcome. Come in. Do not be afraid. I have something to show you. My name is

Claudius". He held out his hand. "Pleasure to meet you".

I couldn't tell if that cheered me up at the time. But finally I thought, "Okay, now follow this man, see what he wants to show you and then get out of here."

I shook his hand back and went up onto the jetty. Only some time later did I realise that that step was one of the most significant steps I had taken in my life.

THE QUESTION THAT CHANGED EVERYTHING

__________The man walked in front of me. His feet were very tanned and very slender, the soles soft and smooth like those of a child. They must have been like this for all the barefoot walking or the sand, which had made his calluses disappear. "At least he saved on the pedicure!" I thought. Anna paid thirty euros a month for the pedicure. My banking brain had calculated in a flash that it was a good three hundred and sixty euros a year.

The wind suddenly picked up. Clouds had appeared in the previously pristine sky and I had the feeling that the jetty was actually shaking. The smell of seaweed, stirred up by the water below us, permeated the air. Only now did I realise that countless ropes and cords were stretched over the hut and also behind it.

Did the connections and the number of ropes follow a pre-defined pattern? I couldn't recognise one. Everyt-hing looked as if it had been put together by a person who wasn't really an expert in construction.

The water shimmered through the cracks in the planks

below me, adding to my feeling of instability. I wanted to get back on land as soon as possible, to have solid ground under my feet. To be on the safe side, I held on to the thick old rope that had been strung as a handrail on either side of the dock.

Years of wind and waves had left their mark on the wharf: a grey-white layer of salt covered most of the surface.

I looked at the sticky salt crumbs in my palm. It suddenly felt numb. Was my hand dry or damp? I couldn't tell. Strange. I was relieved when we reached the wooden hut.

"Welcome to my home. Consider yourself my guest," said the man, letting me enter first. The term house was an exaggeration, because the hut was just a large room furnished with simplicity. In one corner there was a table with chairs and an L-shaped bench, also made of wood. A rather worn, formerly dark blue wing chair with a long footstool stood in front of a small stove. There was also a tiny kitchenette with a worktop. Everything seemed very simple and unassuming.

From one of the windows, I could see the waves now lapping the shore. The water was suddenly no longer blue, but grey. Is it better to return quickly to my accommodation? How long would the storm last?

The wind suddenly began to shake the panes. The fisherman checked one of the windows and shut it tighter. The gusts that whipped the air back and forth were so violent that the ropes outside began to dance.

The squeaking of metal eyelets could be heard right up to the hut. And just to remove any doubts about the opportunity of going back home, the sky sent down a shower, as if it wanted to sweep away the jetty and everything on it.

"Sit down, I'll prepare a herbal tea. It's not time for strolls in the open air now", suggested the fisherman, as he invited me to sit down on the armchair. I hesitated because I still didn't understand what I was doing in the hut. There was a book on a wooden table next to the armchair. „Read a bit until the herbal tea is ready," he said, pointing to the book.

I picked it up. It had a dark red cover. There was no title printed on it, not even the author's name. It was a book of poems. I sighed. Poems just weren't really my thing. I had always preferred watching TV to reading a book. A series on Netflix or an action movie... that was my thing!

"What?" the man asked with an amused grin on his mouth. "You don't like poetry?"

"To be honest, not really," I said, putting the book down.

"Whoever doesn't love poetry, doesn't love life either", he said, more to himself than to me. I decided to avoid a discussion on the matter. He was filling a metal tea

filter with various dried herbs.
"What kind of herbal tea is it?", I asked cautiously. I had once had a severe allergic reaction to a supposedly harmless and very healthy flower pollen tea. I had no intention of repeating the experience.
Something banged against the window outside. The fisherman pulled the hood of the parka he was still wearing over his head and walked out the door. I was alone in the room and from the window I could see him as he was on the dock reattaching some ropes that hadn't withheld the wind. The whole structure seemed cumbersome and even useless to me. Why did people from around here not fish with boats like fishermen everywhere else in the world? Why all this effort?
"There is always something to do! Always something to take care of. There is always a point to focus on," said the fisherman as he went inside and took off his dripping wet jacket. „Did you know that? The place where is called a trabocco. Trabocchi have a very particular history. Around here there are about two dozen." He hung his jacket on a wooden chair which he placed next to the stove.
Meanwhile the kettle on the gas stove whistled. The fisherman prepared our herbal tea and then sat down on another wooden chair next to me. I wanted to offer him my seat, since he was obviously the eldest, but he refused by waving his hand down.

"Stay seated. You need it more than me."
What did he mean? I didn't have time to ask, because he immediately started talking.
"The trabocchi were built to fish without having to go to sea". He smiled at me. "That might seem like a contradiction, right? But it's not. The inhabitants of this region have always been more farmers than fishermen. But they needed more food, because agriculture alone was not enough to live on. The sea had always been there, close at hand. And so one day they had the idea of building this type of boat, which in reality are not really boats. Don't judge the construction harshly!" He told me with a raised index finger, as if he had read my mind. It's very complex, even if it doesn't seem like it. The perfect harmony between the jetty, this hut and the scales - which is the large net that is lowered and raised for the catch - must be meticulously calibrated to resist the fury of the sea".
"This man has read too many poems," I thought.
But I realized that something fully exposed to wind and weather had to actually be flexible and strong at the same time. However, I thought they could have displayed a greater sense of architecture.
"Do you live here?", I asked. Now I really wanted to figure out the kind of person that I was dealing with.
The man didn't answer. He calmly lifted the herb filter out of the pot, carried it to the sink to cool it down,

then closed it with a round lid, filled two big ceramic mugs, and came back towards me. He pushed one of the cups into my hand. "Do you need sugar?"

I answered no with a nod of the head.

He sat down, gripped the cup with both hands and watched the fire for a while. Then a smile crossed his face. "Do you know what I find so exciting about trabocchi?" He looked at me. He seemed to have completely forgotten my question. Perhaps he was already a bit senile?

"What?" "The trabocchi look very wobbly, almost fragile, but they are extremely stable. On the contrary, most of our life out there seems stable, but in reality it wobbles".

„What does this mean?"

"Think about it!" He challenged me.

I found this answer rather out of place, especially since we had only known each other for a few minutes and it was he who had invited me in. He winked at me, signifying that this was his kind of humour. All right... I sipped my herbal tea to buy time, but almost burned my lips.

"Do you mean that someone may appear healthy on the surface, but in reality his body is not?", I asked.

His gaze pierced right through me. It was only that moment that I noticed how light- coloured his eyes were. They were almost no longer blue, and instead

nearly white like the foam of the waves.
He smiled broadly. "Not bad, your answer. You are going in the right direction". For a moment he seemed to stop and think, then he looked at me again. "I think most people out there pretend everything in their life is fine, when they know full well that it isn't. Just keep up appearances! It doesn't matter what is inside you. People wears status symbols, even if they have to go into debt beyond their means". I wanted to disagree, because my job was to grant loans and I didn't find anything wrong with that. He seemed to have noticed. "Did you want to say something?" he asked, looking at me questioningly.
"No", I replied. I had no desire to explain myself to a complete stranger. After all, money can do a lot in life. I would have wanted to get up and leave, but the rain outside would have drenched me in just a few minutes.
"What I mean is that most people pretend not to be afraid. In truth, they make almost all decisions out of fear." The man spoke to himself as if he were simply thinking aloud.
I tried my herbal tea again, which had become drinkable in small sips. What was I to say? I had come here for a vacation. After battling all day in the office with appraisals, ratings, interest rate trends, various other numbers, and not always easy customers, not to mention my boss, my head could use a break. I could ima-

gine that the fisherman felt lonely because he did not meet many people during the day. But was his flood of words it my burden to listen to? It bothered me a lot...
"Haven't you ever thought about that?" asked the man.
"Honestly? No, I have never thought about that," I said, holding his gaze.
"Of course, I only want honest answers from you, otherwise I'll throw you to the fish!", shouted the man, making a movement with both arms, as if he wanted to push me over the edge of the jetty. His gesticulation was followed by a burst of laughter. He evidently found it amusing. I sighed. "So, what's your answer to the question of the day?"
I looked at him confused. "What do you mean? What question of the day?" "The question on the blackboard, right? What would you do, if you weren't you scared?", he replied.
"I'm not afraid," I said without thinking. I thought back to my last mountain bike ride. The paths were dangerously narrow. Some of our group had chosen a different path. But me and two other friends had chosen the "death route", as it was called in insider circles. Even professionally, I had made many courageous decisions and granted loans to companies that had been rejected by other banks.
The man took a deep breath and then exhaled. It sounded like one of those sighs that indulgent parents make

when their child simply does not want to understand. After a few moments, which felt like an eternity, he spoke.

“Even the fishermen back then were afraid. As you may have already noticed, they could have just built boats and set out to sea. But they didn‘t think it was safe enough. The immense sea is very beautiful yes, but it is also a risk to the life of those who do not know it. The fishermen of that time chose the safest route.”

I looked at him questioningly. What did he mean?

“They built these big networks. You drop them at night and pick them up early in the morning, before dawn. Like this, the fish that are around the net end up caught in it due to the current of the sea. But this also means that you only fish what the sea brings. If you went further out, you could decide for yourself what to fish. Do you understand me?”

Of course I understood that, I wasn‘t stupid. His way of being, in a way, was interesting. I had never met a person like him. But there was also something about him that really irritated me. What was it?

I hurried to finish my herbal tea and got up.

“Have you ever felt that you have lost something fundamental in life?” he exclaimed aloud.

“No, that has never happened to me.”, I replied, more vehemently than I would have liked. The man raised an eyebrow. “Sorry. I didn‘t mean to be intrusive.

What are you doing here these days?".
I shrugged. "I tour the area, I rent a bike, I go on a longer tour... Something like that". "Ah, just nice little diversions," said the man with a strange smile.
Was he also conceited?
"Sometimes you just want to run away from your life, don't you?" she asked softly.
"Yes, maybe," I said. "Ok now I have to go". I got up. "Goodbye."
He smiled at me. "Have a wonderful day, Andrew!"
I walked down the pier to the shore again alone, passed through the wooden door and continued on my walk. Or rather, I tried. The conversation with that man had left me pensive. But why? What effect had his words had on me?
"No, I have no fear.", I told myself firmly. "And I won't allow this man to make me fearful either. I am on vacation!"
I thought that the next morning I simply would not have gone to the beach, but I would have done something else. That area was so vast. We obviously would never have met again. But deep down I knew that wasn't true.

**WHAT WOULD
YOU DO,
IF YOU HAD
NO FEAR?**

THE UNSEEN RICHNESS OF LIFE

___________The next morning I woke up at six. The sun was shining and a bird was chirping on my window sill. There was no trace of yesterday's stormy rain. It was a lovely day. But I felt exhausted.

I'd had bad dreams and tossed and turned in bed most of the night. The mattress was not the quality I was used to in my luxury hotels. But that was not the reason. I kept thinking about the conversation I had had with that man. Even though I didn't feel any need to explain myself, I knew I had to go back to see him. There was something still open. Somehow I had the feeling that he didn't believe me when I told him that I had no fear. I wanted to make this crystal clear. I was no wimpy coward!

To wake up I took a cold shower and then I went down to the breakfast room. Even that day there were homemade croissants. This time with a delicious vanilla cream, as the lady at reception assured me. Unlike me, she looked fresh and rested. She smiled at me again in an extremely friendly way. Also that day I ate the croissant, which was actually really good, and drank a cup of coffee.

My eyes sought out that thin strip of sea that was visible from there. You could see a small piece of the pier on which I had met that man. The hut was hidden by a large house next door. Had I thanked him for the herbal tea that he had prepared for me? I no longer remembered. It could have been a good excuse to resume our conversation. I could have pretended to stop by again just to thank him and then elegantly divert to the subject of conversation again.

After breakfast I took the path through the bushes once again. From a distance, the pier looked empty. There was no sign of the fisherman. The blackboard was in exactly the same place. But there was nothing written on it.

Had he deleted the question? Or had it been the rain? No, it didn't look like it. The blank blackboard looked like one from a restaurant where they'd just wiped the menu off. I felt discouraged. Had the man gone as well? And if there were no more questions, were there no more answers? But how? I planned everything so well!

I decided to go and see, and so I walked up to the jetty. The water was very calm, moved only by small undulations towards the shore. The sun gave the rough wood of the jetty and
that simple hut a golden sheen. The landscape looked like a postcard. I couldn't help but think of Anna. I wondered what she was doing in that moment. The previous day we had not been able to speak to each other on the

phone. Maybe she was out with a friend. She often fell asleep on the sofa in front of the TV. I had sent her a good night greeting via WhatsApp, but had not received a reply.

Suddenly, I heard a knock, which came from the jetty. Still no one was in sight. I walked a little further along the pier. The knocks became louder.

Then I saw the fisherman: he was standing on a ladder under the port side of the jetty, banging on a wooden beam with a hammer.

"Good morning, Andrew! Nice to see you again," he said, in a good mood, as soon as he noticed me. He climbed up the ladder and we shook hands. In his other hand, he was holding a hammer, while other tools protruded from his jacket pocket. He brushed a few long strands of hair from his forehead.

"The storm hit really hard yesterday, didn't it?" He looked at me as if he wasn't referring to the weather at all, but to my inner nightly storms and surges of emotion. A moment later he was chatting cheerfully: "As I said, there is always something to do here. But if you take good care of your trabocco, it will last forever. Did you know that some of them are almost two hundred years old?".

I was impressed. "Honestly, I would have never imagined that."

The man nodded. "Do you want to know the secret of their durability?" Indeed, I was interested and expected

explanations about particular technical refinements in the construction of the piers. But what followed, however, surprised me.
"The answer is simple and significant at the same time." The fisherman paused for a moment before continuing. "Gratitude. It's gratitude." He looked at me carefully. "You do not believe me, do you?"
"Well, that seems rather unusual. It sounds very philosophical. I guess it a statement like that will impress tourists who come here!".
He looked annoyed. "What crowds of tourists?"
"Well, for whom else do you keep the shack up and running? You use it to fish, and when you are not at sea, you show people around your house and tells them the same things you just told me."
The man looked at me for a while, then shook his head in amusement.
"You have some interesting thought processes, you know that?"
Now it was I who looked puzzled. "Why is that?"
He changed the subject. "Things aren't always what they seem, my dear. Let's go. It's good you're here, I need a hand!".
He went towards the back of the hut, I followed him. Then he instructed me to help him carry a narrow wooden beam up to where we were standing before.
"Do you know what kind of wood this is?".

I answered that I did not know.
"It comes from the former railway track that ran parallel to the sea". He pointed towards the direction I'd come from with his chin. "The path you walked on to get here was impassable. It was a railway line. Whenever the rails were renewed, the fishermen reused as much material as possible to strengthen the trabocchi. It was a sort of re-cycling, when the term to define it didn't even exist!". He laughed.
Together we placed the beam where he was working be-fore. "I would like to reinforce one of the side pieces. There were some rotten spots. I have already removed the old beam. If you kindly hold the new one from ab-ove, I can tighten it more easily."
I nodded, even though I hadn't gone there to work, much less to do any manual work. But it was clear that he nee-ded help and I had time.
After a short while, he returned with a toolbox and a very basic drill. He masterfully climbed the ladder. He looked like he could hardly stand, which surprised me, since the sea was just a few feet below him. If it hadn't been for the jetty, he would have had the impression of being on a boat, surrounded by waves.
"Thanks for your help, Andrew," he said an hour later, when we finished and he was once again standing next to me on the jetty. We had mostly worked in silence.
"No worries," I replied. I realised I'd forgotten his name

and smiled in a particularly friendly manner, hoping he wouldn‘t notice.
He leaned over the railing and pointed down. “Here at this point you can see the rail parts of the train particularly well, including the nuts and bolts. The fishermen were really clever back then. Everything is made of steel and therefore so durable.”
I remembered the gratitude thing. “I guess the fishermen were grateful that the railway line existed. Otherwise they wouldn‘t have had so much good material.“. I felt very smart. He bowed his head. “Yes and no. I‘m sure you‘re right. I think the fishermen did a lot with the little they had. But gratitude was actually fuelled by the fact that the trabocco provided food for them and their families. Without the fish caught thanks to the trabocco, entire generations would not have survived“.
The rays of the sun, which was already higher in the sky, hit our faces. The heat was good for me and I closed my eyes for a moment. I had the feeling that he did the same. “I don‘t do it for the tourists,” he said suddenly. “I am taking care of the trabocco as a favour to a friend.”
I looked at him.
“The trabocco belongs to him and not to me,” he continued. “I worked in large companies until I retired. And today I lead a different life,” he said. Was I wrong or was there some regret in his voice?
“Would you still like to be on duty?”, I asked then.

"Oh no, no. The opposite! I should have started living this life much earlier!".

I couldn't understand.

He looked at me. "Do you feel gratitude?" he asked me, without continuing with the previous observation.

His question surprised me because there were so many things I wanted to tell him about the fear question. I decided to provoke him a little: "Is this the question of the day? It wasn't even on the blackboard!"

A chuckle escaped his mouth, as patted me on the shoulder. „Yes, you can say that! I like you. So what are you grateful for, Andrew?"

"Well, I would put it differently. So far nothing in my life has magically fallen into my lap. I've always worked very hard to become who I am today." I explained. "In my studies, in the company... I don't think I owe anyone anything".

"That wasn't even the question", he cut me off gently.

A certain anger was starting to rise in me. I had to admit it; I already liked him that day more than the day before. So now the sympathy was mutual. But his frankness bordered on disrespect and exceeded any tolerable limit in a communication between two people, who hardly know one another.

He looked at the sea and said: "You don't have to answer me. Take the question as a gift."

A gift? What did he mean?

He didn't seem to expect an answer from me, but he kept talking: "Back then, the fishermen understood that gratitude is the key and the foundation of everything in life. It is with gratitude that we protect and insure everything we have and are. We should therefore keep gratitude as a precious plant that is very rare and must not wither. At the same time, gratitude attracts wonderful things into our lives, like a magnet. Follow me?"
I stopped to think for a moment. Conceptually, I obviously knew what a magnet was. But I had never heard that it could also be used to attract things into one's life.
"You are not alone, Andrew. Most people don't have an answer to the 'what are you grateful for' question." He glanced out to sea. "They have everything, but they don't realise it. Their existences are permeated by a sense of loss, of nostalgia, of incompleteness. They always feel as though their happiness is not complete. And yet they lacks absolutely nothing! Do you understand? They have more than enough, yet they do nothing or very little! They don't use their full potential! Contrastingly, the fishermen back then had created something wonderful and stable out of old scrap metal. Something that has survived throughout the decades and now the centuries. That's the point.".
I said nothing. His words rang loudly in my head.
"You know, I too was one of those who never found peace for too long. I worked like crazy and earned a lot of

money, yet I lived in constant comparison with those who had more. Which neighbour or colleague had more than me? What else did I have to do or achieve to be happy with myself and all my loved ones? This ongoing competition and the frenzy that ensues is what ultimately makes us all sick. Then, when one adds envy to the mix, everything acts like a sneaky, deadly poison. Envy devours us from within. It dulls our senses, our mind and our emotions. We no longer see what we have, but only what we don‘t have yet. As a result, we shift into an extra gear and push on the accelerator...but without ever arriving at our destination. Because our effort has no real goal. It is never finished because we are never satisfied!".

I thought. A part of me had listened to him with fascination. Another part wanted to run away. Something about his attitude bothered me. He was too close to me. Had he been an old friend, perhaps it would have been different. But I had only met him the day before. I really didn‘t want to explain myself to him. Why was I back? After all, it was my business how I lived my life.

"Well," I said. "Some people want more out of life and others want less. It‘s up to everyone to decide, right?".

He paused for what felt like an eternity. I shouldn‘t have said anything, just said goodbye politely and walked away. Instead of answering, the man looked at his hands for quite a while, turning them slightly from right to left. It was in that moment that I noticed how strong they actually were. Marked by wind and time. Like his face, his hands had many fine and deep lines. He must have been taking care of the trabocco for his friend for quite some time. In my opinion he was between sixty and seventy years old. I wasn‘t entirely sure. Suddenly he looked up as if he remembered that I was standing next to him. “Let‘s sit down. I‘ll make some coffee, if you like.” He pointed to the two wooden chairs sitting on the sunny dock outside the front door. A seagull flew over his head and made a strange noise. He seemed to want to persuade me to accept the invitation to stay.

“Okay,” I said. My heart suddenly started pounding faster, as if I was excited and curious to know what else the man was going to tell me. Why was I so taken in by his story?

A few moments later he came out again with two cups of coffee and a bowl of plain, round biscuits. He pointed to the biscuits.

“My wife and I make them ourselves”.

“Do you cook together?”, I asked amused. The idea of making cookies with Anna would never have occurred to me. Neither of us liked being in the kitchen, and we often ordered something or ate out. My long working hours didn‘t even allow for grocery shopping and cooking.

„Yes. We started a few years ago.”, replied the man. He

bit into a biscuit. "Help yourself, taste them! They are very good.".

They really were good. The simple shape was deceiving, but the taste was fantastic.

"They were made with a lot of love", said the man with a smile. He winked at me.

"Tell me about yourself," I asked him. I could not explain why my interest in this man grew more and more.

He took a sip of coffee. "Well... where do I start?" He thought for a moment. "Perhaps like this... I've always been a nature lover. I was born here, not far from here. Since I was a child I dreamed of being a fisherman. I wanted to sail with a boat across great seas, but my father expected me to do ‚real work', as he called it. He wanted me to be a bank manager. He too was employed in a bank, but not as a director. I was the eldest son and following my father's wish was the right thing to do, or rather, that was what I believed at the time.".

"That is crazy!", I exclaimed. "We have one thing in common, I work in a bank too!"

He raised his hand and smiled slightly. "Be patient, be patient."

I felt scolded and a little rejected, but a part of me understood that he wanted to finish the story.

He continued: "I studied business administration. I was doing very well. I was one of the best, and I finished my studies faster than I expected. Later I met Rosalia, my

great love, who later became my wife. Thanks to my father's connections, I got a good job in a well- known bank immediately after graduating. I went up the ranks very quickly and became department head. With this 'safe base' and a good salary I was able to marry my Rosalia. She stayed at home, as did my mother, and she took care of our children, Fabrizio and Stefania. I've always worked a lot, so Rosalia often had to take on my role as a parent. It can be said that she was both mother and father to our children. But she never complained: she always had my back and was very happy about my successes at work. Together we celebrated every step of my career, which kept on improving..."
He stopped and looked at me to see if I was following his storyline. Of course I was listening. I would never have even remotely suspected that that man, who looked like a simple fisherman, had a path behind him so similar to mine! How easy it is to be deceived by looks.
"Then, one day, a large energy company contacted me and hired me to work for them. I earned more, had a higher position, and worked even more than before. From that moment on, I started staying in the office on the weekends; during the week I usually didn't come home until eleven at night, when the children were already in bed. I was the CFO. I was accountable for many employees, and I had an enormous amount of pressure on my shoulders every day. I've always wanted to do my job

well, indeed, perfectly, I would say. After all, I was been put in charge of the finances of the whole company. I also wanted my father to be proud of me, of my career, which was what he had wanted for me. Sadly, my father was not one to show how proud he was of me, but I think he was.“

The man became very thoughtful. “Well, sometimes it is like that, isn‘t it? You perceive the expectations of others, and you try to satisfy them all. But, one way or another, it is never enough. So, you work even harder! Until you realise that you‘ll never be happy, because it‘s not success that makes you happy, it‘s not the salary, it‘s not the job description on your business card. What matters are the people you can share all of this with. This is so much more. The people you live with.”.

I nodded. We were both silent for a moment. I could hear the gentle lapping of the waves hitting the edges of the jetty. I inhaled and exhaled the salty air deeply.

When the man looked at me, his expression looked brighter again. “The people who have made me really happy in life are my children and my wife. Fabrizio and Stefania are wonderful! The best children a father can have. And Rosalia is the most amazing wife I could wish for, and beyond that, a great mother.“

“What do your children do?”, I asked. I realised that this question was always the first one that automatically came up: the question about your profession. But why?

Why didn‘t people ask, “What kind of people are your son or daughter? What does he or she like? What sense of humour do they have?” ... strange.
“Fabrizio is a very talented basketball player, which makes me very happy. I always told him: ‘Do something you like, because I do something I don‘t like all day’. Fortunately, he listened to my advice. And my daughter? She followed in the footsteps of my mother, and those of her mother: she raises her children with a lot of love. And she has a husband who works very hard every day, who is always incredibly stressed. It’s an old song that seems to repeat itself with every new generation...”. He looked at me and raised his eyebrows. “Yes, that‘s how the years went by, up until the moment I retired. Sometimes I wonder why I didn‘t realise earlier the madness I was experiencing. Spending so many hours a day, a week, a month doing something for the company and customers, but then not even having the time for a walk to the beach with my family in the weekend! Do you understand? I had no hobbies or friends, although I may have had a few because my old school friends kept contacting me to meet up. But I never had time for them. Instead of spending time with my closest friends, I occasionally invited business partners on Saturday nights. Rosalia was an excellent cook and, despite the busy week with the house and the children, she prepared delicious food for us. While we men talked, Rosalia chatted with the

other wives. I didn‘t realise at the time that she would have much preferred to go out just with me, or to have a day off. I only realised it when it was too late. Today I think: ‚How blind have I been? Where was I directing my attention? What was I focused on?‘."

He inhaled and exhaled deeply and rubbed his eyes . Was he crying? No. But the lines around her eyes and mouth had deepened. I didn‘t dare speak. Not even swallow. His words moved something very deep inside me.

He looked at me. "Do you have any children?"

I shook my head.

"You are married?"

"No, but I‘m in a relationship," I replied.

"Ah...an affair", the man muttered, lost in his own thoughts.

"What did you say?"

"Nothing, nothing. My daughter, with whom I have always had a very strong bond, often asked me: ‚Dad, why do you work so much? Why don‘t you ever hug mom? Why are you always so silent? Are you sad?‘." He shook his head with a smile. "Her questions were so wise. The soul of children is often wise."

I wanted to cheer him up a little, because I noticed from the slumped shoulders that his memories were weighing heavily on him. "Well now you do have time, and you can do something nice with you wife whenever she wants", I said smiling at him.

"Unfortunately, that is not the case."
"What do you mean?"
He looked at me insistently, as if he wanted to pierce through my soul. His eyes suddenly looked much darker than the day before. Dark blue like the sea. Deep. And deeply sad.
"My wife is very ill. She can no longer leave the house."
"Oh, I'm so sorry.", I said shocked. I did not expect him to say that.
"It's okay. Do not worry. How did you know that?" He stared off into the distance for a moment before continuing. "I think she could no longer bear the life we led. In the last few years before retirement, she was increasingly depressed and exhausted. She was bedridden for a long time, she had to take very strong drugs and we had to look after her from morning till night. Sometimes she reacted, sometimes she didn't. Then came the first symptoms of paralysis. At first, she was able to get up and walk a few steps, but suddenly that was no longer possible either. She is now confined to a wheelchair. We have arranged the house so that she can move independently.".
He sighed deeply and I too had to catch my breath. I really couldn't believe what he was saying. It hurt me just hearing his words.
"I know. It's not a happy ending. Now that I have all the time in the world, I can't spend it with the woman I love

with all my heart, like I‘ve dreamed of doing all these years. It‘s too late.”.
He leaned back. He took a few deep breaths, almost as if she needed to catch his breath after that story.
I did not know what to say. There was no correct or appropriate response to such a story. I had often considered my life to be difficult. But compared to that man‘s story it was a bed of roses.
I wanted to comfort him, reassure him by saying: “But you can nowadays... I mean, there are so many places without architectural barriers...“
“What a stupid thing to say!” I thought as I said it.
He wasn’t offended, but merely shook his head.
“Rosalia doesn‘t want to, even though I have repeatedly offered to do it. With the wheelchair, it‘s not as easy as it used to be. Well... that‘s why we decided to make the best of the situation. So now we cook together! Bread, pastries...everything edible. We like to try things. Different ingredients, different types of flour. You have just tasted the result. These are made with spelled!”.
He held up a cookie, looked at it from all sides and suddenly smiled at me again, radiantly, as if we had been casually talking about the weather and about cookie recipes.
I had a lump in my throat that hurt. “Honestly, I don‘t know what to say”, I confessed after a while.
“Then don‘t say anything.” His sight nonchalantly gla-

zed over the sea, as if he was simply enjoying the beautiful day. It seemed as though he was feeling better. His demeanour had shifted from grave and gloomy to unexpectedly light in a flash.

I was extremely confused. I thought of those glass spheres in which, when you shake them, a whirlwind of small snowflakes falls. It always takes some time for them to sink back to the bottom and for the image to become clear enough to distinguish what is inside. At the moment, I was not able to distinguish anything. Why had that story touched me so much? I hardly knew that man. He looked at me as if he had guessed my thoughts and wanted to give me some clarity. "This is what I mean by gratitude, Andrew. Gratitude alone gives things eternal life and their proper value. Be thankful for what you have. Just let go of all external striving and pause. So much of what we think is important is actually completely irrelevant. Never forget that."

He stood up. "I'm sorry, but I'm very tired. You're welcome to stay. Or go for a walk," he said kindly. "If you go a little further that way, there is an enchanting bay. And thank you again for helping me today!"

He grabbed my hand and squeezed it tightly.

"I wish you a wonderful evening. See you tomorrow!". He smiled at me.

WHAT ARE YOU GRATEFUL FOR?

FRIENDSHIPS BEYOND EXPECTATIONS

__________The next day my knee pain had gone away. I decided to go jogging after breakfast. I took the road that led exactly to the opposite side of the trabocco. I needed to be alone for a while.

The man's words and his story kept buzzing in my head. I was amazed that he had opened up to me so much. Did he do this with other people as well? He really didn't seem like the chatty type.

"See you tomorrow," he said, as if we'd already made an appointment. Did I really have to go back? Or was I putting myself into a situation that I would never get out of? I didn't usually make friends that easily. Certain people pretended to hang out after their first meeting and assumed that they would spend a lot of time together. Especially after I told people what I did for work, sooner or later, they all used the excuse of having a beer to ask me for advice on how to make profitable investments.

But with the man on the wharf it was very different. What he said and did always sounded like an invitation. I didn't have the impression that he wanted to impose his presence in any way.

I went for a walk along the coastline for more than two hours, with the sea on my left hand side, enjoying the sun on my face, the salty air, the light-heartedness. No email had lit up my cell phone.

Once I arrived home, I took a shower and felt suddenly exhausted and refreshed at the same time. Life coursed through my veins. It was a fantastic feeling. From the lady at the reception I learned that there was a place nearby that made really good food. She showed me the path to take to reach that small family-run restaurant on the map. To get there, I had to walk in front of the trabocco. If the man had been there, I could have quickly greeted him. I would think about how to continue the afternoon while I was eating.

Meanwhile, the sun had risen a little more and it was pleasantly warm, not too much. This was the weather I loved while I was on vacation. I tried to imagine the wonderful lunch I was about to enjoy. Perhaps a multi-course meal? Something special, like a nice fish? It could also be a bit expensive. I had worked hard enough in the past few weeks and felt the need to reward myself.

When I passed in front of the jetty, I realised that there was something

different compared to the previous days. In front of the hut there was a long table, six people between the men and the women. The white tablecloths gleamed in the sun. I heard laughing. They were toasting to something.

I was about to keep walking when the man came out of the hut, saw me and waved: „Andrew!".
He came towards me smiling. On his shoulders she had a kitchen towel. He was wearing a white shirt and beige pants. As always, strictly barefoot.
A couple of people at the table looked in my direction.
"How nice of you to come!" said the man, still standing a couple of meters away from me. "Come. Let me introduce you to my friends".
I refused. "Another time. I do not want to bother. I still have a few days left!"
I wanted to turn around to leave when he said to me: "No, no. You are not intruding! On the contrary: we were waiting for you. There is a free seat for you at the table. Come on, join us!"
In the meantime they had all turned towards us and were looking at us curiously. There was no way to get out of it. Okay. I would have tried the restaurant that the lady at reception had recommended another day. I walked up onto the jetty and returned with the man to the table.
"Everyone, this is my friend Andrew," he said at the table.
"Hello Andrew!" said the two men and three women, all of different ages. Lots of friendly faces were looking me. „Pleased to meet you. Come, sit with us!".
I was a little unsettled by the fact that the man had in-

troduced me as a friend of his. We barely knew each other.

"Hi," I said softly with a small nod of my head.

"I will be right back. They will take care of you," the man said, winking at me, as he disappeared into the hut.

"Take a seat. Come here next to me so you have the best view of the sea," a man around forty-five said kindly to me. He had thick dark hair with the first streaks of gray. His eyes were also dark and lively. He waved me to the empty seat on the bench to his right. "I'd even have you sit you next to my wife," he said, as he pointed to the pretty brunette woman sitting to his left, "But sometimes she bites, just like that, without warning. I can't take this responsibility. At least not on our first meeting!" Everyone laughed, and I with them.

"I'm Toni," he said and held out his hand.

I shook it: "Hi Toni. I am Andrew. Pleasure to meet you."

"I am Lucia", said the dark-haired beauty beside him. "And of course I don't bite. Evidently, my husband wants you all to himself." She held out her hand, smiling.

I shook her hand promptly: "Pleased to m make your acquaintance, Lucia".

Lucia gave her husband a pat on the shoulder, after releasing my hand. "What are you going around saying to people..."

Toni laughed, grabbed her hand and kissed it lovingly.

Next to Lucia sat a young woman, with straight black hair that reached down to her chin. She was wearing a light blue blouse that she had knotted at the waist just above her jean shorts. She, too, gave me a nice warm smile.
"This is our daughter Laura," Toni said introducing me. I nodded to her: "Hello."
"Then we have Aurelia", continued Toni, looking at the lady at the head of the table, "who is the youngest, the fittest, and the most creative of us all."
She was joking again. Aurelia was certainly not the youngest. She must have been about seventy years old. Her shoulder-length gray hair was neatly trimmed. The simple, flowing pantsuit she wore and the pearl choker was very elegant. She held her torso remarkably straight, as if she'd been doing ballet or yoga for years.
"Thank you, my dear Toni, but you are exaggerating once again", she said, winking at me cheekily. Her gray eyes looked very wise and soulful.
"Nice to meet you, Andrew." I too gave her a friendly nod. "It's a pleasure for me as well." Aurelia vaguely reminded me of a client I had looked after a few years earlier. She was running an art gallery at the time. I had visited her once in her gallery and was surprised at the effect her large paintings had had on me. They made me think, even just about the use of strong colours and unusual combinations in the art... Even in the bank offices,

there were one or two works of art hanging on the walls, but none of them were as thought provoking as these.
I began reminiscing about the time I was in high school. Back then, I was quite good at drawing and had made some amusing cartoon-style caricatures of our teachers and classmates. For a while, I had taken into consideration taking a painting class. But a couple of friends teased me and said painting was for girls. So I discarded the idea forever.
"And at the end, or the beginning of our little introduction tour, depending on how you want to see it, here are Maria and Domenico!". Toni pointed to the couple sitting across from us. They were more or less the same height and width, I thought to myself, amused. Not that they were fat, but they gave the impression of being robust and well built, like two people who have always worked hard in life. As for age, they must have been around sixty- five years old.
Maria wore a light blue shirt and a thin gold chain with a cross around her neck. Her cheeks were lined with many small wrinkles, like those of her husband. Domenico had rolled up the sleeves of his plaid shirt to his elbows. I imagined them cultivating fields of vegetables or on an orange grove.
"Maria and Domenico are our Adam and Eve," Toni said, introducing them with a smile. „ I think that they were already in love and married before this place exis-

ted! And they still are!"
The two laughed. Domenico pulled Maria towards him and gave her a kiss on the temple. "And you know Claudio," Toni said, pointing towards the man who was leaving the hut once again. That's what his name was... Claudio! I never had to forget it again. Claudio was carrying a large tray of appetisers. There were several dishes featuring anchovies, olives, sheep's cheese and slices of tomato with mozzarella, which all looked very enticing. In the middle, there was a basket with fresh bread. I got up and helped him distribute the plates and bread in the middle of the table. He thanked me and brought the tray back inside.

"Can I pour you some wine?" Toni asked and pointed to my glass as I sat down again. They had really been waiting for me, I thought. How could Claudio be so sure that I would come back?

Then I realised I still hadn't replied to Toni. "Yes, gladly", I said, still a little perturbed. "What are you waiting for? Come on, my friends, help yourself. Enjoy your meal!". Claudio, who had just come out of the hut again, placed a large salt and pepper shaker on the table and then he sat down with us.

He was seated to my right, at the head of the table opposite Aurelia. The two smiled at each other. There was something familiar and warm in their gaze. Something friendly.

I wondered if I too had female friends, the equivalent of a male companion or a male friend. The answer was immediate. No. I had been with several women, but no friendship was ever born. Why was that?
"To you, Andrew!" Toni said, as he raised his glass towards me. And with a look at the whole group: "To us all, and to our health. Cheers!" Everyone participated in the toast. „To love and passion!“ cried Domenico.
I also wanted to contribute. "Success!" I shouted. Glasses clinked. My gaze met Claudio‘s. He looked at me for a moment, as if I‘d said something totally inappropriate. Or was it my impression?
Everything that Claudio had prepared was very good. The olives, the tomatoes and even the cheese and the anchovies, everything had a fragrant and very genuine flavour. I was surprised by how much I liked everything. Was it just my impression or was the flavour much more intense?
"Do you know how to tell if a black olive is authentic?", Toni asked me. He had pierced a sample with a fork and was holding it up.
"I didn‘t know there were black olives that weren‘t authentic", I replied "Now I‘m curious. Shoot."
Toni bit off a piece of the olive and showed me the inside of the fruit. "This is a real one. It has been ripening in the sun for a long time, so it turned dark by itself,

almost purple. Her seed is green, see? The false ones, on the other hand, change color by oxidation in a chemical bath. If you look closely, even the seed turns black. And they are always very uniform black on the outside, while naturally dark ones have some irregularities. Their skin doesn‘t tan perfectly on all sides."

"Like those on the beach who set the alarm every thirty minutes to turn over on the sun bed“, Laura interjected cheerfully. Her parents laughed, as did Domenico and Maria.

"We should try to turn the olives in the sun...", exclaimed Domenico. Aurelia also smiled. "I‘ve learned something again," I said impressed by the olive story. "I have to remember that."

"Tell us a little about yourself, Andrew. What do you do in life?", Lucia asked.

I assumed they were asking me about the job. "Let‘s say," I began, "that I make sure that my customers‘ best and most valuable things grow." I consciously paused to wait for the reaction of my listeners. I read on their faces that they didn‘t understand me.

"Their money," I added.

"Ah, then I‘ll come and see you too! Don‘t forget to tell me where you work afterwards, huh?" Toni exclaimed and they laughed. "Sorry, I didn‘t mean to interrupt you."

"No problem," I said with a smile. "I am employed in a large bank as an asset consultant. People who have liquidity of a few millions come to me, and they want to know what they could do with the money before the next economic crisis sends everything down the drain."
I was trying to be funny, but I noticed that no one was laughing. Maria leaned forward to better look at Claudio. "Then he does what you did, Claudio, right? You have something in common" and she smiled.
Claudio nodded his head. "Well, we actually have a lot in common." Again he looked at me. "However Andrew deals with another calibre of people. At least financially speaking." He smiled at me and Maria. Maria nodded.
I looked at him carefully. What did he mean? But he didn't continue on that line of conversation.
Before I could think about it further, Lucia interjected: "Money or no money, I think the most important thing is that you like what you do."
"I think so too," Maria agreed. "At that point it makes no difference whether you come back late at night or work on the weekend. But when you have to do things you don't like, any hour or moment of the day becomes heavy. If you despise something, you never find the time to do it".
On this matter, they all agreed.
Claudio handed me a bottle of red wine. "This one is very good. It comes from a friend of ours, Giovanni.

Unfortunately, he is no longer with us, but his children have carried on taking care of the vineyard. And so Giovanni also continues to live on with us." Everyone nodded in loving memory of their friend.

I thanked him, poured some into my own glass, and handed the bottle over to Toni.

"To Giovanni!" Toni shouted, after he and the others had poured themselves some wine. Everyone raised their glass.

"He was a wonderful person," Laura said, as she looked out onto sea. "If it weren‘t for him, I wouldn‘t be studying today. Sometimes people say one sentence and that sentence changes your entire life."

The atmosphere was getting a bit heavy and I thought about how to intervene. Dark moments weren‘t my thing. Smiling, I said: „When Anna, my fiancée, five years ago asked me to move in together, well... that sentence changed my life!“.

Everyone retreated out of the remembrance of Giovanni and smiled.

"Yes, women sometimes really mess up our lives". It was Tony.

"You do too, and not to a small degree!" Aurelia answered without hesitation, raising her eyebrows in a playful way. More laughter.

"Do you have children?" Lucia asked.

I shook my head. “But I have three grandchildren. They are my sister‘s daughters. We don‘t see each other often, but when we do it‘s always very nice.”
Lucia and Maria nodded with a smile.
“Children are such a wonderful thing,” said Maria.
“And what do you do when you‘re not working, Andrew?” asked Aurelia. His intelligent eyes landed intently on me, as if it were just the two of us sitting at the table.
His question irritated me a little.
“What I meant to say is, what are you interested in?” he said coming to my rescue. Ah, he wanted to know about my hobbies.
I felt Claudio‘s eyes on me again, but I didn‘t turn around to look at him. I twirled the wine glass between my fingers for a while as I thought of a good answer. “I really work a lot, even in the evening and on the weekend. When I‘m free, I gladly go on special trips, walks, skis, mountain-bike excursions...“
Toni seemed to like my answer. He nodded smiling: “A nice ride on a mountain bike sounds really nice”.
“Do it,” I advised him. “I can give you and your friends a couple of insider tips.” With a wink in her direction, I added, “Women stay at home, of course. We men need to be with each other once in a while, have real man talks and all that,” I said with a smile.
Toni barely smiled. Was it possible that he had never

gone out without his wife? Oh lord!

I looked around. The others listened attentively. Their faces were as open and friendly as they had been that entire time.

"Of course. Conversations with the right people are very valuable. Man or woman," Claudio said approvingly. It was the first time that day that he had said anything similar to

the things he had said in the previous days. I almost missed his philosophy. I felt the urge to smile.

"I recently read something very interesting," shared Laura. "They say that our footprint and our attitude are the sum of the five people with whom we spend most of our time. Can you believe it?" I was surprised by the thoughts she had.

"Well, we were all lucky then!" exclaimed her father. "But, wait..." He pretended to count all the people sitting at the table with his fingers. He went around three times and each time he started with the seat next to his left: first with his wife, then with his daughter, then with Aurelia. Wherever he started, there were always two left at the table. "So I'll have to think about whether I'd rather be the sum of you here, or you, or you..." He thought about it for a moment and laughed. "I think all combinations look good on me!"

We all joined heartily in his laughter.

Lucia came back to the main holiday theme and started speaking of her last winter trip to South Tyrol with Toni. They went skiing with a small travel group and Lucia had probably had a hard time on skis. After two days, she preferred sitting in a cozy café and wait for Toni and the others in the group with a nice coffee and some delicious cake. It seemed as though she didn't mind. "You always have to make the best of every situation. This way, I was finally able to read all those books that I would never otherwise have been able to read". She smiled at the table.
A memory flashed through her mind. "I was also in South Tyrol in the winter three years ago", I shared before anyone else could intervene. "Among other things, I almost died!" I said, noting that I sounded almost a little proud that I was so close to death.
"Oh God, that‘s terrible! How did it happen?" Maria asked. Her gaze was genuinely concerned and I suddenly regretted bringing up that episode. The atmosphere, after Lucia‘s story about her coffee, desserts and books, had been pleasantly light. They all looked at me with some tension. I had to finish my story.
"Well, let‘s say that I thoroughly enjoy skiing off the main ski slope", I said. "One area of the mountain was closed off, as there was a high risk of avalanches, but I had to go and check it out. The view was absolutely magnificent. I thought: ‚Come on, Andrew, you can do

it!...But I definitely took too great a risk! I went down a hundred meters, without any protection!"

I spiced up my narration with a gesture of the hand that descended rapidly downwards. "Fortunately, my comrades were able to quickly organise a rescue intervention," I continued. "But let me tell you: you really do believe that your last hour has come when you're barely hanging on the mountain wall like that, with your snout – pardon, your mouth – full of snow!" I smiled apologetically at the ladies in the group and took a sip of the red wine. "Thank goodness you're still here, otherwise we wouldn't have met you today!" Domenico said, toasting and taking a sip too.

I looked at him and felt a feeling of unknown happiness. How precious his words sounded. I couldn't help but think about my friends back home. No one had ever seen it that way. Until now, others I'd told this story to had listened intently, but they'd often made ironic or even sarcastic comments immediately afterwards. "Oh, Andi". I liked Domenico's way of seeing things.

I felt Claudio's gaze on me, so I turned towards him. He didn't say anything, but I had the feeling that he was looking straight into my soul. What was he thinking right now? I had no idea.

He immediately looked away and asked everyone: "Does anyone want a coffee?".

His offer was well received. Laura jumped up to help

him and disappeared with him into the kitchen.
During the afternoon the conversation topic had gravitated around the weather, the olive harvest in autumn, the upcoming village festivals, some amusing incidents that Maria and Domenico had experienced with their grandchildren... We didn't talk about anything in particular and I realised that this was exactly what I liked. Just a relaxed conversation between friends. Not having to pay attention to what was being said. Not having to look for the sensational thing to tell. All without competition and without ostentation.
I perceived myself taking more deep breaths and felt my body pleasantly relax. I could have sat there forever with those people. How strange... I didn't know them at all.
After enjoying a strong coffee, Toni reached under the bench and pulled out a guitar. He sang some simple melodies that sounded very touching. After a while I was able to sing along a but too, even though I didn't know the words. Laura had an extraordinarily beautiful and powerful voice. She and Maria smiled at one another as they sang.
Every now and then, while she was singing, Lucia put her arm on Toni's back and stroked him in a gentle, delicate, discreet, not at all clingy manner. I liked it a lot. All faces at the table beamed. What a beautiful moment, I thought. And how natural it was for them to sit here and just be happy.

The afternoon flew by way too quickly. The sun was approaching the sea and it was starting to get cold. It was time to leave the tents. Together we cleared the table, washed and dried the dishes in Claudio's kitchen and put everything away for him. Everything went smoothly, without quarrels, discussions or who knows what agreements. Everyone just did what was needed. I noticed that not a single bad word had been said all afternoon; no strange looks, just openness, friendliness and warmth.

'Even at home my friends and I have always had a lot of fun.' I thought. But there were also some strange moments. The people Claudius was surrounded by, on the other hand, were simply unreserved. Yes, that was the right word for it. They welcomed whatever that moment or that person put on the table. A new experience for me. When we parted, Claudio smiled at me as if he had read my thoughts. "Hope you had fun with us, son." It was the first time he had addressed me so affectionately. And at that moment I felt I wanted to finally abandon my formalisms, which were a sort of useless barrier. I nodded. "It was really a wonderful day, thank you so much for inviting me. Thank you to all of you!" I said a little louder so that the others could hear me. They nodded at me.

"Come back to see us", Toni exclaimed, closing the kitchen cupboards. "We would love that very much." The

others nodded. “Very much. And bring your Anna!”.
I nodded too. Yes, that was a good idea. Anna would have loved to be there with them too. With the pleasant sound of music in my ears, I returned to my apartment elated. Hadn‘t Claudio spoken of gratitude yesterday? I felt so grateful in that moment, from head to toe! The friendly reception lady was still arranging some paperwork when I passed. She smiled as soon as she saw me, lifting her gaze. “Good evening. Nice to see you again! How did you find the restaurant? Did you like the food?” “I ate really very well. But not where you advised me. I ate at the trabocco. I was invited,” I told her. She nodded, as if she already guessed where I‘d been. “Ah, so you have been taken hostage by Claudio? I can imagine. And how did it go?”
“Extraordinarily,” I said without thinking much. “A truly very special day!”
She nodded again, smiling.
Hearing Claudio‘s name, I was reminded of something. “Excuse me,” I said, “Would you like to tell me your name?”
For the third time she nodded, pleased. “Of course. I‘d love that. My name is Rosa Maria”. “Really a beautiful name”, I felt like saying. “Good night, Rosa Maria. Ah... and my name is Andrew”.
“Pleasure. Goodnight, Andrew,” she said amicably.
“I almost forgot to say...,” I said turning back to her, “...

it is really very nice to be your guest".
„Thank you! I'm so glad to hear that," she said. „See you tomorrow. Have a good night". I suddenly felt terribly tired, but in a pleasant way. The long walk in the morning, all the afternoon in the sea air... But I still had the desire to hear Anna's voice.

She was very happy when she answered, she heard my voice. She listened attentively to my entire account of the afternoon at the trabocco.

"You have a really nice voice," she said just before starting up. "I can't wait to hear all the things you tell me about."

She didn't sound at all like she held anything against me, unlike the other times I'd traveled alone. When we hung up after kissing goodnight, I sank into the pillow. I suddenly realised that you don't need a three-course meal to feel happy and satisfied.

I didn't feel like watching television that evening. I had enough good stories in my head. Stories told by life. I started reminiscing on the stories told by Toni, Lucia, Laura, Aurelia, Maria and Domenico. I suddenly realised that I hadn't asked for anything. They had asked me many questions and had been very interested in me, but I hadn't asked anyone anything. What was Giovanni's sentence that had changed Laura's life? I wanted so much to know. Too late.

I felt like I learned something really important.

I was almost a little ashamed that I hadn't lived up to my new friends, even though none of them had given me reason to think so. Everyone had always responded warmly to what I had said, to the Andrew that I had been. I decided that next time I would talk less and ask more questions. And maybe this was a good thing to do at home too.

WHICH PEOPLE MATTER TO YOU?

THE UNWRITTEN MESSAGES

__________The following morning, after breakfast and a brief and pleasant chat with Rosa Maria, I immediately set off towards Claudio and the trabocco. I was relaxed and in a good mood, even though I was a little annoyed at a customer‘s email.

I couldn‘t help but take a quick look at my inbox. The message came from a gentleman who was always very resolute and demanding, difficult to please. It seemed as though he did not realise all that my colleagues and I were doing for him and his good fortune. Every attempt to communicate with this man was a power struggle. The ideal would have been to read or hear absolutely nothing of him.

Why had I looked at the emails? "My bad," I thought. It was difficult for me to ignore my cell phone in the evening, on the weekend, or on vacation... I tried to avoid the thoughts and emotions associated with what I had read as best I could. The long run the day before had left me with no sign of muscle soreness. On the contrary, all my joints felt pleasantly loose. I could feel the wind gently brushing my hair. While shaving, I also noticed how good the salty air was for my skin. I felt 'smoothed' inside and out, even though I'd only been there for three days. Small birds were chirping in the bushes along the path and I thought I could hear the buzzing of bees too. Were they there the day before? I hadn't noticed them. I entered the trabocco. I wanted to thank Claudio again for the previous afternoon. It really had been nice. I could have invited him to the restaurant Rosa Maria had recommended. While I was thinking these things, I crossed the catwalk towards Claudio's hut.

But he wasn't there. I knocked on the door, but no one answered. "Claudio? Claudio!" I called loudly, and looked down both sides of the dock to see if he was fixing anything. Or maybe he was having a morning swim in the sea? No, he was nowhere to be seen. Next to the door there were only the two wooden chairs. One was empty, the other was a book. The sun beat down on the chairs. The whole scene was inviting and at the same time was reminiscent of a theatre stage setting, the only difference being that here there were no actors. Maybe Claudio had only gone away for a moment and he would be right back? I could have waited for him for a while. Since I had nothing else planned, I went to the chairs and sat down on the one on the left. The book on the right was Claudio's book of poems. I recognised the dark red cover.

I allowed my gaze to drift aimlessly. The sea was almost still below the dock. It appeared as a large blue silk scarf

with iridescent tones, which stretched gently towards the horizon.
For a while I focused my eyes on that calm blue. It reassured me. Strange, at home it would never have occurred to me to sit around and do nothing. I wondered how long it would take Claudio to get back. I clearly couldn't wait for him for hours. A seagull landed on the dock to my right and looked at me with its head cocked to the side. I thought about the fact that seagulls can never see what is straight ahead of them. They always give you either the left eye or the right eye. "So what?" I said to the seagull.
He tilted his head away and curiously took a few steps towards me, but kept a safe distance. He was probably hoping for something to eat, because he opened his beak and made a guttural noise, as if to say: "Come on, throw me something!"
I shook my head. "I have nothing for you, my friend. I am sorry."
He still stayed with me. He probably didn't have anything better to do in that moment. Time went by. I was starting to get impatient. Would Claudio have arrived or not? What time was it? Reaching in my pocket, I realised I'd left my cell phone in the room. Damn! I couldn't even check what time it was. How long had I already waited? Ten minutes? Half an hour?
The seagull inclined his head again as if to ask: "And

what are you doing now?"

I did not know. I hadn't made any particular plans for the day. I was in no hurry. However, I was losing patience. I sighed. I would have given Claudio a few more minutes; if he hadn't come then, I would have stood up and left.

My gaze rested on the book. Between the pages was a handwritten piece of paper. Could it be a note from Claudio for me? I took the book and opened it. The note said: "Awareness is the purest and rarest form of generosity." What did that mean? I didn't have the faintest idea. However, it didn't seem like a message from Claudio.

I closed the book and put it back on the chair. Claudio was a peculiar man, very different from all those I knew. But I was happy to have met him. I would not quickly forget the afternoon of the day before.

The conversations I had had with Toni, Lucia, Laura, Maria and Domenico, their openness and warmth, their unprejudiced interest suddenly flooded my mind.

I couldn't help but think of the countless training courses I had already attended. "Show interest in your customers", they so often said. "Put yourself in the customers' shoes. Ask them questions."

Honestly, who was really interested in customers and their needs? Wasn't it always and only about the goal after all? Weren't the questions merely aimed only at

closing the deal?
You didn‘t learn to be genuinely open and friendly. Now I understood it. Despite this, it was curious that I had been very successful. But was that really enough, I suddenly wondered? Wouldn‘t it have been so much nicer if there had been more than just a shared affair? A new quality? An authentic union? A common basis of trust and the certainty of being able to count on the other at all times, both as a client and as a consultant?
My questions surprised even myself. I had never made such reflections.
Something inside told me that I wanted to start building again from that moment, from that afternoon with the others. I didn‘t know how yet, but I wanted to try.
The seagull came a little closer.
"And you? What do you do out and about all day?" I asked jokingly. „It is certainly much easier being a seagull than a human!".
The seagull opened its beak and made its guttural sound again, as if to say, "Do you have any idea what a seagull‘s life is like?"
I felt the urge to laugh, and I stood up. The seagull watched me intently as I walked from the chair to the edge of the jetty and leaned against it. There was still no wind. I ran my hand over the wood. It was still hot from the sun, dry and powerful.
I couldn‘t help but think about Claudio‘s words, about

the countless and varied materials that the fishermen had been reusing for decades and centuries to build and stabilise the trabocco. I imagined what our bank and insurance buildings would have looked like if not only new and modern materials had been used to build them, but also materials previously used elsewhere, which had proven their great qualities. Unimaginable, but also interesting. Now that would have been conservation of resources and the environment, not just an empty slogan written on a banner.
Once again, I marvelled at my own thoughts. I extended my arms above my head and did some stretching. Then I looked at the sea again.
Is it perhaps that by continuously talking about "my house, my boat,..." we were actually very far from nature and from our true selves? Somehow we all needed a sense of belonging. I looked down at the seagull and he looked at me, as if he had guessed my thoughts.
"And where are your house and your boat?" I asked him. The seagull kept his gaze fixed on me. "And how many Followers do you have on Facebook or Instagram?". I smiled at him. "You have no idea how great your life is!"
I thought about the cell phone, which was in my room. How many times would I have looked at it in times like these, checking emails, scrolling through social media, playing some silly game? Certainly several times.
And now? Had I perhaps missed something? Had the

world collapsed because I hadn't looked at it? No. On the contrary. I wasn't even bored. Normally, boredom or pointless waiting killed me. Instead there, in that moment, I felt rather calm. And excited. Yes, both at the same time, although it might seem like a contradiction. This trabocco was a rather interesting place. I was starting to like it.

Still no trace of Claudio. The beach was empty. Had something happened to him? Maybe his wife wasn't feeling well. Did they have to go to the doctor? Did his children need him? Had he received unexpected guests? Or was he just resting after having been with friends? My initial anger was beginning to give way to these thoughts, and a slight worry start to creep in. Whatever had happened, he surely had a good reason not to be there that day, I thought. We hadn't exchanged cell phone numbers. I didn't even know if he had a cell phone. Even if he had wanted to warn me, he wouldn't have known how.

Only then did I realize that we didn't actually have an appointment. Just because we'd seen each other three days in a row, I'd assumed he'd come back that day too. But he wasn't. It was just my expectation. And this expectation was not fulfilled. This made me angry. Even if nothing had happened at all.

I remembered other situations in which I had gotten angry in a similar way, when something didn't go the way I wanted it to. I was known for not being a fan of waiting, and for expressing my disappointment out loud when things suddenly changed and I wasn‘t warned in time. I had often had arguments with colleagues, friends and also with Anna because of this.

But had I ever tried to listen to what the real reasons were? No, I had to admit. I just didn‘t care. I got angry. Full stop.

The phrase on mindfulness from the note in Claudio‘s book came to mind. One thing was sure: I certainly wasn‘t going to meditate three hours a day in the future. But the idea of greater awareness appealed to me. The thought of looking at things with greater depth, understanding what was behind them, asking myself questions about the real reasons, being more helpful and caring towards other people.

I thought about that morning’s email. What was the real reason that customer always behaved this way? What was the customer trying to tell me? And above all, what was I communicating to him? Was I giving him reason to behave like that towards me?

The thought made me uneasy and I didn‘t want to elaborate on it further. But a voice inside me told me that, if I really wanted to change something, I could no longer look for excuses as I did before. Maybe I should have just asked that man to share his thoughts on how the collaboration with me and my colleagues was going, and

what he really wanted? Yes, that could have been a good start.
The seagull suddenly flapped its wings as if to give me a signal that it was time to go. Then he got up and flew away. I watched him fly further and further away into the distance. I had betrayed his expectation of getting something to eat from me. But I still hoped that he would have enjoyed my company. My stomach began to rumble. The sun was high in the sky. Was it noon already? Suddenly I was filled with a great desire to try that nice restaurant, and maybe even order spaghetti with clams. After all these thoughts and reflections, which were unusual for me, I really deserved a nice lunch.
In a good mood, I walked back across the wharf. The wooden chalkboard caught my attention. The day before and the day before that, it had been empty. Yet I took a look at it. Incredible. This day it had words on it, written in chalk.
Had Claudio passed by? The sentence was a question, once again. I took a step towards the blackboard and read:
"What would your life be like without distractions?"
I turned towards the dock. The two chairs in the sun were empty again. The book placed above one of them. And I could almost see myself standing there at the end of the pier, looking out to sea.
The spaghetti on the restaurant terrace were heavenly. I

was more than satisfied and had the sensation of perceiving the flavour of every single ingredient, like the day before with Claudio's friends. I looked around. Even the people sitting at nearby tables seemed happy.

They listened attentively to one another. I saw gestures of love. Hand-holding. A strand of hair gently pushed away from the other person's forehead. Smiles that didn't limit themselves to upward arching lips, but that lit up the eyes and hearts of others...

Once again, I marvelled at myself. I was amazed to perceive so many different things than before and to even find the words to describe them.

I wondered where all this would take me, smiling. Anna would have hardly recognised me, if I had told her all those thoughts. But something told me that she too would be very happy with my experience and my evolution.

Suddenly I felt completely at peace. I was sitting there, alone at my table, yet I didn't feel alone. On the contrary, I was in excellent company: my own. That evening I fell asleep with a profound serenity and joy which I hadn't felt in a long time.

WHAT WOULD YOUR LIFE LOOK LIKE WITHOUT DISTRACTIONS?

THE NET AND THE CATCH OF LIFE

__________I woke up with a pleasant feeling. That morning the wind as stronger and the weather less beautiful than the previous days. As a result, I preferred to have breakfast indoors. I could see the sea in the distance pushing little crowns of white foam through the large panoramic window. I was still keen on walking to the trabocco. I wanted to see if Claudio had returned.

Rosa Maria wished me a good day as I passed in front of her. Today she was friendly as always, but quieter than usual. For a moment I thought about asking if she was okay, but then I didn‘t. I grabbed my jacket from the room and walked.

Thick gray clouds had gathered in the sky. You could no longer hear the birds and the bees in the bushes. Surely they had sought shelter and were waiting to see if there would be rain or a storm.

When I got to the dock, I saw that something new has been written on the blackboard. So Claudio must have at least made a pitstop at the trabocco.

“Are you living your dream?” was written on the blackboard.

Are you living your dream? What an absurd question! Millions of consultants had dealt with this. I hadn't read any of their writings, because I had always thought they were one of those terrible neo-spiritual things. Anna had suggested a few years earlier that we do a seminar together on our dreams and life goals, but I had refused. I didn't see myself in a circle of chairs among people who let out everything they are feeling, and who share with anyone their deepest feelings and desires. Those kinds of scenes reminded me of the movie scenes wherein the protagonist attends a self-help group and everyone smiled at him compassionately.
In the worst version of my imagination, joss sticks were lit, everyone wore colourful scarves, and everyone had to dance their emotions. No, that kind of soul striptease wasn't for me. I'd rather leave it to others and rather meet friends for a beer after work. "At least you always know what it is," I thought with a smile, as I tightened my grip on the collar of my jacket. The wind had picked up again, the waves slapping against the edges of the dock. A particularly high wave splashed up to the boards I was walking on. The wood was getting wet. I quickened my pace before the next wave hit and kept walking.
Claudio was kneeling on the ground at the beginning of the jetty with his back to me. What was he doing there? In a day as grey as that one, he was barely distinguishable with his silver hair, dark jacket and linen trousers.

"Here you are at last! I was starting to think you weren't coming anymore," he muttered as I stood next to him. How absurd! It was he who hadn't come the day before, not me! I wanted to tell him, but I held back.

Claudio looked angry. He reluctantly tugged on one of the three-foot-long tethers of the large rectangular net that hung deep in the water. Only the outermost edges were visible and if the net had not been reinforced in the centre with a large piece of stronger white cloth, it would not even have been noticed due to how transparent it was. From our height I couldn't see how many fish were swimming in it.

„Give me a hand, come on! It's stuck," Claudio said, brusquely.

Oh, what a nice greeting! I sighed and squatted down. We leaned forward.

With a wave of his hand, Claudio ordered me to free a string connected to the net from a screw. The vine was sticking out of one of the wooden beams and the noose was wrapped around it. I obeyed. While Claudio lifted the net slightly, I untied the tangle. Done!

He let go of the tether and stood up. "Thank you. And now let's see what we caught!" He walked over to one of the two upright wooden poles that were set into the walkway near his cabin. Both were about two meters tall. I had noticed them since day one, but until then I didn't know what they were for. Four shorter beams were attached to each of the poles, about chest height, and radiated from the main pole. They looked like the spokes of a large wooden wheel.

Claudio put his right arm around one of the spokes, pressed his entire body weight onto it and began to spin. The whole pole rotated in sync and the rotation moved the net into the water, which rose very slowly. What a clever mechanism!

I deduced that the other pole belonged to the other large net that had not been lowered into the sea that day. It floated about two feet off the surface of the water and was empty. A kind of net was attached to a pole about five meters long, which was probably used to retrieve the catch from the net and bring it to the overflow. Simple but effective! However, all together it did not seem capable of catching large quantities of fish. I was curious to see what would appear in the net below.

It took quite some time and many turns before Claudio lifted the net enough to see the bottom of it. A few fish - not many - of different sizes and colours wriggled in it. A net so big, that it must have been five meters by five, for that pile of fish? It seemed to me a really small catch. But I said nothing.

Claudio fixed the pole so that he could not go back and ran to the point where the net was hung. Without speaking, he showed me how to use the net to get the fish out of the net. Every now and then a fish slipped away.

Inside I sighed. Surely they didn‘t do big business that way! But I didn‘t want to distract him, so I remained silent and tightened the collar of my jacket just a little tighter.

The thrashing fish, the foaming waves crashing against the jetty, the wind tugging at our jackets and tossing our hair—it all lent an adventurous quality to the moment. “It‘s not a relaxed job, being a fisherman,” I thought. “Long live my hot, dry, air-conditioned office.” “Go get that basin over there”, shouted Claudio suddenly. With a quick nod of the head to the shoulder, he pointed to the hut, while still holding the net with both hands. There were three black plastic basins set to one side. I followed his order. They seemed to have been in use for a long time. They were scratched in several places and exposure to the sun and salt had also left their mark.

“Put the big one there!” He yelled into the wind, pointing to a spot marked with a white cross in the middle of the jetty.

“The other two go to the right and to the left of the one you just put down. We put all the fish in one and then sort them after!”. I understood and pushed the three basins side by side where he had asked me. Meanwhile Claudio carefully retrieved the long shaft of the small net. There was a great stir in the dark web that now hung between us. From below, water dripped into the basin.

"Attention, now comes the best part!", said Claudio. He was suddenly relaxed and friendly again. His eyes lit up and he winked at me. With one deft movement he twisted the net and the fish dropped into the large basin amid splashes and wriggles. Some of them stood still, others wagged their tails.

They were either silvery, bluish, or a grey-brownish colour. Beautiful animals! I usually bought fish in some delicacy department. I found it lying there, already cleaned and artfully displayed on large chunks of ice. But this was something else entirely!

Claudio looked at me and smiled. It was evident how much he loved this activity. "Sorry, I was a bit rude before. This part of the job always requires a lot of energy and concentration".

"No worries" I said. I knew those moments when you had to concentrate very well. There was just no time for words and being tactful. But I realised that I was not used to being on the other side. I was usually the one giving the orders or distributing the tasks. The others - my colleagues, my friends - often suffered my disappointment.

At the time I was disturbed by Claudio's greeting. Knowing full well that it was not up to me but to him, which he had just confirmed, I asked myself unexpectedly: was this how I too wanted to appear to my clients or my team members? To Anna? No, not really. But was it

even possible to avoid it in the stressful everyday life of the office? And how?
“Come on, come on!”, Claudio interrupted my thoughts. “Look, we even caught a tuna today”.
He boldly walked over to the basin and pulled out the tuna. The fish was almost a meter long and seemed to weigh a few kilos. I had only seen tuna canned or presented as a sliced steak, seasoned with olive oil and lemon.
The animal Claudio was showing me was beautiful, silvery, with dark fins.
“Usually you only catch them far offshore. But this was carried by the current,” Claudio said happily. “I‘ll roast him for lunch if you like.”
I accepted with enthusiasm. „I would love that”. My mouth was watering just thinking about it.
“We also have squid. They are enough for a good soup“.
He continued to explain particularities of the other fish we had caught as we distributed them by size in the two smaller basins. The squid went into a bucket that Claudio had filled with water. He put the tuna to one side.
Each type of fish had something special. I never ceased to be amazed while Claudio spoke: how they were prepared, with which types of wine and side dish they were best served with ... he seemed very competent in the matter. I already imagined him as he happily experimented with new recipes with his wife.
He straightened up and stretched his back for a moment.

"Camillo and a couple of other friends will come later. They need the fish for their shops and restaurants," he said.

"So you get to have a little second income from fishing," I said.

Claudio shook his head. "I don't take any money for this."

I looked at him amazed. "Why not?"

"Because I have what I need. I don't need any more money", replied Claudio. "When you have enough, you have enough. Chasing even more money is a deception and a futile enterprise, one in which many people get chained for life". He smiled. "I give my friends the fish they want and once in a while I stop by and have something to eat, alone or with my family. The math doesn't always have to add up, you know?". He gave me one of his stinging looks, which I knew well by now, to see if I understood what he was saying.

Of course I understood, even though the banker in me gave a gasp of rebellion. But I just had to smile. I liked Claudio's attitude.

"But how did things work for the fishermen of the past years and decades?", I asked. Claudio had taken the large basin, now empty, and had carried it up to a pipe attached to the outside of the hut. "What do you mean?" He asked me, looking at me sideways. Meanwhile he took the hose, turned on the water and gave the basin a quick rinse. Then he leaned it against the wall of the house to dry.

I took a few steps towards him, because the wind kept muddling every word I pronounced, and I didn't want to have to shout.

"Well, you said the tuna ended up in the net today, even though it doesn't normally happen this close to the coast. In fact this means that you can never predict what and how much you will catch". Now I was standing next to him. Claudio straightened up and gave me a long, scrutinising look before speaking. "Right. Well said," he said. "This is both the blessing and the curse of the trabocco". He wiped his hands on an old cloth and handed it to me as well. Curse? How could he speak of a curse, when this orchestra of posts and nets, sophisticated down to the last detail, had been in operation for hundreds of years?

Once again, a gust of wind blew our jackets. He caught the net near us, its handle swinging dangerously back and forth. He gestured for me to go with him.

"Let's put everything in its right place. Otherwise it will break. You take care of the net, I will deal with the small net". He pointed to the wooden post. "If you go in the opposite direction, it will go down again". Realizing, I wrapped one of the spokes under my arm again, pressing my body weight against it, and began to move

counterclockwise. The net sank very slowly, until it merged again with the sea and until only the edges protruded from the water, just as it was before.
In the meantime, Claudio had put the small net back in his place. It was again suspended above the net and could not get out of its support.
"What did you mean by ‚curse' just now?", I asked shortly after, when Claudio was next to me again. He had helped me block the post.
"You don't have to do anything. The current carries the fish," he explained to me. "You must not go out there and expose yourself to the storms and waves, to the danger and power of the sea, which belong to the sea as much as beauty does. This is the blessing of the trabocco". He paused for a moment. Then he continued: "But you also have to take what comes. Sometimes the current brings you something and sometimes it doesn't. Sometimes a lot. Sometimes not much," he continued. "Even if a huge fish swims within a few meters of your net, you won't catch it! Because the network has a fixed location. It stays where it is, always. It doesn't move. You cannot say: 'Today I will throw it a bit further out', but you can always and only take what enters the action space of the network". He traced the rectangular shape of the net in the air with his hands. "That's the price you pay when you choose to fish safely. Out there," he pointed out to sea, "there are far more fish, far bigger, heavier, more

extraordinary, than you‘ve probably ever seen in your life! In comparison, what we have caught here today," and he pointed to the two basins that stood nearby, "is very modest. But to have the rest, everything, you have to go out to sea. Until you do this, you will always have less than what is possible. Did you understand? You live only a part of the dream, but never the whole dream."
I remained silent and reflected on his words.
"The farmers of that time had no choice," Claudio added after a while. "They weren‘t fishermen. So they found this compromise. They fished safely! And, as you can see, shore fishing works, but it‘s not real fishing. But we, now, unlike the fishermen of the time, can choose. You and I".

I felt caught on the spot. "But you are the one who always talks about gratitude!", I erupted with a certain vehemence. "One could simply be grateful for what the current brings. No?“ He laughed. "Ah, you‘re trying to beat me at my own game. Very good!" He wagged his forefinger, smiling a little mischievously, as if to reprimand me: "You are absolutely right, my friend, but one thing by no means excludes the other. What I mean is that most people limit themselves. They are afraid to go out to sea. But since they don‘t want to admit that they are afraid, they convince themselves that they are doing everything right. In reality, they are not living the life

they could actually be living. They are not satisfied as they would like to be. They are not really free, even if they think they are!". He looked at me. "Are you with me? Do you understand what I'm trying to say?"
I shook my head thoughtfully. "As far as I am concerned, I can say that I am living exactly the life I have always wanted".
Claudio looked at me seriously. "Really? Or have you simply never asked yourself the question that underlies everything?".
"What question?"
"The question of what else might be possible". I felt his eyes penetrate my eyes and my soul. He made me uncomfortable, so I looked away. We remained silent for a while. I looked towards the sea. Many things whizzed through my head, like the waves that swelled and fell agitatedly beneath us. The wind had gotten stronger. I pulled up the hood.
"You know, in the end, we are all shaped by those who came before us", I heard Claudio exclaim. "Our parents and grandparents were full of good intentions! After all, safety is an important element of existence! But with all this certainty, many forget to live and how much life can still give us! How many truly make it? How many can look back and say: "This journey, my life journey, has been magnificent! Think about the great inventors, the brilliant minds, influential pioneers we read about today

in history books or on the internet. Every one of them set sail. They went out to sea. Were they afraid? Oh yes, definitely!" His voice took on a warning tone. "But they chose not to let fear govern them! They courageously pushed forward, leaving behind the easier path of hypothetical security. They followed their dream."

I felt his hand on my shoulder and I turned towards him. His face was wet. Was he sweaty? Or was it some water that had dripped onto his face from the net earlier? Or was he shedding a few tears? I couldn‘t tell. But I sensed his emotion and it infected me, whether I wanted it to or not.

"A ship is only safe in the port, Andrew! But she wasn‘t built for the port." He took his hand off my shoulder, took another look at the catch in the basins, and walked over to the cabin. I looked at him for a moment. The smell of sea salt suddenly became more intense and also the smell of fish... I felt the dock under my feet. Fishing safely... Had I done that too? And to what extent? Claudio took another step towards me. The wind had died down a bit and the volume of his voice went back to normal.

He sounded almost tender when he said: "Thank you for helping me. Enough for today. Now we really deserved a nice herbal tea. What do you think?" I nodded.

Thoughtful, I followed him into the hut. Claudio closed the door behind us and I sat down on the wooden bench, while he went to the stove to put water on the fire. It was as if there was still a question out there on the wharf, waiting for me, that wanted an answer.

ARE YOU LIVING YOUR DREAM?

WHEN UNTYING THE KNOTS

__________When I woke up, I remembered the dream I had that night. It was unusual for me. Normally, I could never remember what went through my head at night. In the dream I was in the mountains with Claudio. The fisherman had taken me on a mountain bike tour. It made me smile to think that, of all people, it was a fisherman, who rode a bicycle in the mountains. At the top of the peak was my father, standing as if he were waiting for us. I remembered my amazement. What was he doing there? We had never been in the mountains together. He looked happy and smiled at me as he rarely had in real life. How the hell had he gotten there? With his old scooter? With the car? Neither of them were could be spotted. Apparently, Claudio and my father knew each other. They hugged like two old friends and laughed together about something that I didn't understand. They spoke too softly. I remember in my dream standing there confused and thinking: "I guess I'm in the wrong movie".
My father beckoned me to approach him, put a hand on my shoulder, pointed to the valley and said: "Look,

Andrew, you can only fish what the current carries!" He stretched his hand, pointing to the valley that stretched deep below us. I followed his hand with my eyes, but I saw nothing. No water, no fish: only the valley and other mountains around.
"But there isn't even a creek here", I told him. "Where should I fish?"
Claudio replied. He was standing next to me on the other side and said, "That's exactly the point. You have to leave the mountain and fish in real life, Andrew".
It was when those word were spoken that I woke up and I laid for a while, confused. Fishing in real life? What did that mean?
I had no idea, but it had made me surprisingly happy to see my father in a completely different light, more relaxed and free than I had ever seen him. "It's crazy, the things that happen in dreams!" I thought. And that it was my father, of all people, who met me in the first dream in my life that I actually remembered ... If I told Anna! She often dreamed very intensely and she was then able to tell me everything in minute detail. A few years earlier she had read a book on dream interpretation and she had given me some examples of symbols and explained their meanings to me. At the time, I thought it was a lot of nonsense. But at
least, on my way home, I too would have had my first „real" dream to tell about.

The thought made me smile.
That was my last day there. The week had flown by so quickly. The next morning I was supposed to drive back to the airport. All the more reason to experience something truly beautiful again that day! With this in mind, I took a quick shower and went towards the main house, to the breakfast room, all the while in a very good mood. The croissants looked even more delicious than the previous days, in which they had already been exceptionally good. I had breakfast inside because there were more guests than usual outside that day on the terrace and I preferred to be by myself. Rosa Maria seemed a little more rested again.
She was very busy with the numerous guests who presumably had arrived the night before and were constantly wanting something from her. So I tried to be especially nice, which she seemed to notice. When she refilled my coffee cup, glancing at me to see if everything was okay, a smile crossed her face.
Just as I was about to get up and say goodbye for the rest of the day, she came over with an oblong parcel wrapped in brown paper. „You‘re going to Claudio again, aren‘t you? Could you please bring him the sandwiches?"
Her question surprised me. How did she know I‘d go back to see him? But since, in that moment, another guest was already calling her, I didn‘t have time to ask

her anything. Then I nodded quickly: "Of course". She gave me the sandwiches and wished me a good day. Then, she immediately turned her attention to the guest. For a moment, I stood there, puzzled, with the package in my hand. Then, I nodded to a couple at the next table and went back to my room.

I had, indeed, planned to go to Claudio's again that day. But how could Rosa Maria know that? I had only told her once about meeting with him. How well did they know each other? Had they talked about me behind my back? And if so, what had they said? Question after question, my brain was flooded with words, as I took my backpack from the room and walked towards the sea. Did the two of them plan on me meeting Claudio from the beginning? No, it couldn't be true. Or maybe it could?

I thought back to my first meeting with him on the dock, the storm immediately after, the herbal tea in his hut ... I suddenly felt uncomfortable and I didn't even know exactly why. At home, in the company, I was always the one who knew everything, even what happened behind closed doors. I realised that not knowing something made me feel insecure and even irritated.

"Now stop it, calm down", I said, reassuring myself. "How can you think such things about them? They're nice people and it's probably just a coincidence. Maybe they are also somehow related and you have nothing to do with it".

It was true: neither Claudio nor Rosa Maria, since my arrival, had ever given me reason to doubt them. Maybe I was just hallucinating. Like tonight in the dream. A little calmer, I went up to the jetty. And I stopped. What had happened? Countless nets and even some ropes lay scattered on the wharf. It seemed that a storm had broken loose. But the beach didn't look like it had been battered by a storm at all, I said to myself after a quick look around. Besides, if there had been a storm at night, I would have noticed. If there had been a heavy downpour and a strong wind, the shore would have been filled with seaweed, branches and other things brought in from the sea.

Instead, the beach looked clean and well kept, and the sea was very calm. That mess on the dock amazed me even more.

It was at that moment Claudio came out of the hut. He smiled when he saw me holding the package. "That's nice, you brought it. Thank you very much!"He didn't go into further detail, but he took the sandwiches and carried them inside the hut. When he left, he said: "I'm sorry for the mess today, but it is absolutely intentional". He smiled.

What did he mean?

"Today we have a task that is as important as fishing itself", he explained to me. "We check and repair the nets," he added when he noticed my questioning gaze. "Or rather... I'll fix them, but if you want, you can gladly give me a hand".

Only then did I notice that in one hand he was holding a roll of strong thread and two large needles, about four inches long, with oval eyelets, reminiscent of the shuttles used in weaving.

He tossed the spool of thread lightly into the air and caught it again. "If the nets are not intact, there is no fishing. Or, at least, there is a worse catch than what you could potentially get. Even through the smallest holes, the fish can find a way back to the sea, and so all the effort made becomes useless. That is why regular care and maintenance of your equipment is so important. They are the basis for good fishing."

I nodded. I understood what he was saying. "And how long does it take to repair a net like that?", I asked. For my last day of vacation, honestly, I would have hoped for more exciting activities.

Claudio smiled. „It takes as long as it takes. Have you ever mended the nets?".

I shook my head. Fixing nets had never been on my "one hundred things to do before I die" list up until that point."

"I can teach you, if you're interested." Without waiting to see what I thought, he walked over to the net that laid further from the hut on the dock. I followed

him, in a rather demotivated spirit, and crouched beside him on the boards. They were dry and warm from the sun. A light and pleasant wind swirled around us. Claudio took a knife from his shirt pocket, cut a piece of thread and threaded it into one of the needles. While he held the needle between the fingers of his right hand, he slipped a piece of net between the fingers of his left and searched the stitches for tears and holes. After a while he found what he was looking for.
"Look, only a very small link has come off here. But if I stick my finger through it, there's enough room for a fish. And where one can come out, many can come out".
He showed it to me. "And zac! They're leaving, faster than you can watch!" I nodded.
With deft movements and a few well-aimed stitches, Claudio mended the net. If the thread hadn't been darker than the net, you wouldn't even have noticed at first glance that it had been mended. Seeing Claudio doing this reminded me of the crafts lessons the girls had in the sixth grade at our school. We kids had technical education lessons and we could let off steam with wood, paper and metal. Meanwhile the girls sat in the classroom and worked with knitting needles or crochet hooks and with intricate patterns. "How glad I was to be a boy!" I recalled with a slight smile.
Claudio, on the other hand, didn't seem to mind this

chiselling work. He was calm and very patient, hardly saying a word, as if he too was immersed in his thoughts. "Here, you can try now if you want," he said after a while, as he handed me the second needle, the spool of thread and the knife. I cut a piece of thread, threaded it through the eyelet, and slipped a section of netting through my fingers, as I'd seen him do before. I actually spotted a loose knit and was proud of it. You almost had to look at these little links with a magnifying glass. I had already forgotten how Claudio had stitched it up.
Looking at him to it, it all seemed easy. He noticed my hesitation and showed me the threaded seam again, as well as the stitches on a new hole he had just discovered.
However, the stitches were far from precise and I was about to say: "I don't have girl fingers!", but since Claudio also had very strong hands, that shouldn't have been the problem and I kept my mouth shut. However, my first result was not very brilliant.
I sighed: "In all honesty, I'm not at all sure that I'm not contributing to make the hole bigger than it was before," I said. My neck was sore in that uncomfortable sitting position, and I felt a great resistance to the thought of how many meters of net were still missing. However, I decided to take courage and not give up.
Once again, my father came to mind. Why had I

thought twice about him that day? First in the dream, then, right there, on the dock. Unlike me, my father was a good craftsman and mechanic. When he was young, he was able to fix his old scooter himself. He never went to a repair shop. He had assumed that he had passed on these skills to me, but he was quickly proven wrong. I had no desire for all those greasy gears. I preferred being alone or with my friends, riding our bicycles, compared to being dragged around clouds smelly of exhaust fumes, also because I knew nothing about engines and carburettors. Mechanics simply didn't interest me, neither back then, nor now. The mechanics simply had to work. How it worked and how something was fixed - I preferred leaving that to others.

"Yes, sometimes it's a struggle!" Claudio laughed.

I looked up. Had he read my thoughts, as he often did, or did his statement just refer to fixing the holes? I did not know.

He winked at me. "Relationship work: was all he meant. "Repairing the nets is like repairing the tears in the web of our life".

"I'm sure you'll now go on to explain to me what you mean by that too," I muttered under my breath. And indeed, after working in silence for a few more breaths, the explanation came: "Our life is made up of many connections and ties. We are connected with our family, with friends, with our partner, children, colleagues, superiors, and all the other people we meet in the course of our lives“, Claudio began to explain. “A lot of connections you take for granted, right? Some are stronger, others weaker... But which of us ever thinks of analysing, taking care of and maintaining them on a regular basis, as we are doing with the nets, here, right now?

From time to time, it is important to stop and examine even a relationship, which perhaps is strong and lasting, and ask yourself: is everything still okay? Is it still solid? Has it cracked or is it missing something? Was there an event or conflict that perhaps made the network penetrable? Am I missing out on so many good things because I didn‘t pay enough attention and didn‘t mend my web in time?”

He raised his eyes briefly and looked at me with his piercing gaze. I must have looked puzzled, and indeed I was. I had never thought about the networks in my life, as he called them.

He continued: “Every conflict, every unpleasant situation, every resentment that we carry within us can cause a tear in our network of relationships. One very small or one deep and punchy. All things with which we haven‘t made peace in our lives they weaken the network and therefore we, ourselves, become weaker. Our strength, energy, joy can escape through those

holes, just like a beautiful moment... And if the network is too worn out, then one day our entire existence will also be in danger, because the network no longer supports us. You know what I mean?".
I nodded. As always when he talked about life in his own way, I was having a little trouble keeping up with him. But something in me shared what he was saying.
"And, as you see from what we're doing here today, it's about work. No one said life is easy, right?". A short laugh escaped his mouth.
"For example, I myself have thought for many years that I have something to prove to my father," he continued. "When I compared myself to him - which I often did, unfortunately - I never felt good enough. I always believed that what I did was never enough in my father's eyes.
So I always wanted to do better and show him that I was a good guy, as they say. But no matter how hard I tried, it was never enough. Never! He never told me he was proud of me. That is why today it is so important for me to repeat this to my children over and over again. Do you understand?
Fixing nets can also mean addressing things. Even if this doesn't always heal and repair them. But just by speaking, we have a chance to change something.
Silence, at times, only makes wounds more profound."
I gave him a quick look, but he was busy searching his

net for other holes to fix. I did the same. I was suddenly reminded of a sports competition from my time at school. It was just before the 8th grade summer break, and the event was a great opportunity for us students to show our parents what we had learned during the year. I was very good at athletics and I came in first in the hurdles. I proudly showed my parents the medal and diploma I had received at the awards ceremony. Of course, the medal wasn‘t made of precious metal, but I felt great for the rest of the day and put it back on before going to bed at night.
There was no praise or even appreciation from my father. Later, my mother scolded him for it. She embraced me affectionately as if to compensate for his inadequacy, but his affection could not appease my desire for paternal approval. Why hadn‘t I just told my father that his silence had hurt me?
I thought about sharing this story with Claudio, but the busy silence that reigned between us was pleasant. I didn‘t want to interrupt him. We continued to work side by side.
It surprised me how much Claudio trusted me. He didn‘t once check the stitching I was doing. The only thing that interrupted our silent activity was a seagull that landed near the railing. He greeted us with a guttural sound. Wasn‘t it the seagull that had kept me company a few days ago, when I was alone on the

dock? Perhaps.
Somehow these birds all looked alike, but something in his eyes reminded me of our meeting. Claudio put down the net and stood up.
“I’ll make coffee. Do you want some?“
“With pleasure”. He declined my offer to help him in the kitchen. Instead, he pointed to a mess of tangled rope lying nearby. The ropes showed traces of seaweed and salt. They must have been in the water for a long time.
“We can also work on knots. If you need a break from stitching, see if you can untangle that tangle there. If not, I‘ll have to buy a new string. But I‘d like to use it again,” he said to himself, walking towards the cabin.
“Untying the knots is not too difficult,” I thought. I stood up as well and stretched my back for a moment which had stiffened from sitting still.
Then, I grabbed the net and examined the knot from all sides. At least the strings weren‘t as delicate as the net, but some of them even had a diameter of two or three fingers. I would certainly have untangled it before Claudio had time to return with the coffee. At least, that was what I assumed.
Nope! After tugging and shaking it a bit, I realised that the tangle of strings resembled one of those puzzle games that required extreme puzzle skill to find the solution.

When Claudio returned, carrying a tray with two cups full of coffee, some biscuits and a large knife, I hadn‘t untangled it by even an inch.
“Is the knife for the biscuits or the knots?” I asked jokingly, setting them down and helping him set the tray on the floor.
Claudio replied with a smile. “The biscuits will melt in your mouth, my friend. Today they are made with almond flour and pistachios. Help yourself!” I handed him one of the cups, took one for me, and served both of us a biscuit.
“So, how‘s the Gordian knot?” he asked while chewing.
“You did it on purpose. Admit it!” I said with a slight smile. “It is not humanly possible to undo it”.
“Of course it is!”
He said, indignantly. “The knots didn‘t tie themselves, after all! Somehow they have taken shape over time. And, therefore, it is possible to retrace the road backwards. So? Are you giving up so easily? I really didn‘t expect that from you.”
I sighed, took a big sip of coffee and took a bite of my biscuit. It was very delicious.
“Let’s just say that” he said with his mouth full.
“Worst case scenario, I brought this knife with me. But it would still be very good and extremely useful if you at least tried it first and see if anything can be

done. You must know that I am attached to the old ropes as well as to the nets. Replacing them with new ones is possible and would be faster. But first of all, it's an additional expense and, secondly, it is against the principle of trabocco".

I didn't understand it right away, but then I thought about it and said: "You intend to reuse everything as much as possible".

He nodded with satisfaction. "Exactly. You have a really good teacher.

What's his name?"

We both laughed.

After having finished our coffee and cleaned the plate of biscuits to the last crumb, we sat down together again.

"I'll give you some advice," he said, as I laid the tangle of ropes in front of me, trying to figure out which end I should work on again. "Do it slowly," he said. "The faster you pull, the tighter the knot gets. Everything hardens and you lose even the last hope. At that point, a clean cut is the only way to go".

Was I wrong or was he talking about life again? He didn't say anything else on the matter, but continued: "You have to find the crucial point. The real cause of the knot. If you don't see it right away, you have to work on it calmly." His finger pointed to a point in the knot. "In my opinion, this is the crucial point. This is where the chaos starts. But I could be wrong. Give it a go".

I had no idea why he pointed to that spot, but I attributed it to the fact that, unlike me, he had already untangled some knots in his life.

Claudio also took a rope. And again, when he was going it, it all looked very easy. Wow. How did he pull the ropes through the knots so effortlessly?

"Wouldn't it be nice if there weren't any rips in our webs and no knots in our lives at all?" He asked, unexpectedly. I had the feeling that he was trying to provoke me.

"Just imagine what kind of life we all would have then... everything sorted out. Everyone at peace with themselves and with others... Total serenity... Isn't that a wonderful idea?"

I nodded. "That is just not everyone's definition of life, sadly, right?"

He nodded. "Yes and no. I think most people don't even think that they could try to live that way, and that it is actually possible. But you must start somewhere. You have to take the first step, even if it often seems to be the most difficult." He swung a piece of rope up and down.

„Wiggle the end of a knot back and forth a bit and see if anything changes. Many people give up before they even start. Like you just did!" He winked at me, turned serious and continued to fiddle with his knots. Then he continued. “Obviously, a broken relationship can‘t be mended in just one weekend. And, of course, it is not easy to apologise to someone after thirty years or more. And why not? It‘s better than all of us dying and taking all the unspoken words to our graves.”

I reflected on his words. Once you put it like that, it makes sense. I had never thought about it. With whom did I still have a few knots to untie?

Surprisingly, as soon as I asked myself this question, an old classmate immediately came to mind. We had always teased her at school because she was quite large and she wore glasses that we considered for geeks, with big and thick lenses. Then she got a job at an insurance company three blocks from my bank.

Sometimes, during the lunch break, our paths crossed, but she never said hello.

She had become much prettier and she no longer wore glasses. She could see me and still turned away, pretending I was see-through and that we had never met. It never really got to me. But now that I thought about it... Was there anything I could do? Would she have accepted an apology so many years later?

What if she wouldn’t? What if she would?

I involuntarily smiled.

In that same instant I looked at the tangle of rope on my legs and thought: “It doesn‘t matter how long it

takes. This isn‘t about being the fastest or the biggest. Just untie one knot at a time. Try until you can no longer find a way out. You always have time to cut ropes. But that‘s not why you‘re here, is it?"
My own inner voice surprised me.
Where did it come from?
"And what about with your father?" the same voice asked me.
"What about with my father?", I asked again. But no answer came. Not yet.
I don‘t know how long Claudio and I sat like that. As if it was only us, the pier, the nets and the ropes. The seagull had already taken his leave some time ago and had flown away.
At one point Claudio stood up and said: "I‘m going to get the sandwiches you brought. Relationship work makes you hungry, huh?", he winked at me and walked towards the cabin.
Shortly after, as we bit into Rosa Maria‘s sandwiches, stuffed with delicious ham and cheese, I felt happy and strangely light-hearted, as if a knot had burst inside me that I didn‘t even know I had.
"You‘re leaving tomorrow, right?" Claudio asked, breaking into my thoughts. Amazed, I looked at him.
"How do you know that?"
For a moment the unpleasant feeling of unease that I had had in the morning when Rosa Maria had handed

me the rolls returned to me. Had she told him about the length of my stay?

This was about invasion of privacy. The organ of inner control - the one, which I so often needed in my work - took hold of me. A moment later, however, I was proved wrong.

"I do not know. I am guessing" Claudio said in a low voice, shrugging his shoulders. "This man is and will always be a mystery to me," I thought.

"I hope I didn't get on your nerves too much with my stories, and that you still enjoyed your holiday!" he exclaimed with a smile.

There was a mischievous glint in his eyes. He smiled and I shook my head.

"On the contrary. I really enjoyed your cookies. And not only those". Claudio nodded, serious again.

"It has been like that for me as well. Shall we meet tomorrow to say goodbye?". The way he asked the question sounded unusually cautious and prudent, contrarily to how his remarks are usually - quite brutal and direct. As if too much frankness could break something between us.

"See you," I said. "There is no way around it." We both laughed.

As I crossed the gangway back to shore, I suddenly felt a slight pang in my chest. No, it was nothing physical. I knew exactly what it was.

I was sorry that the next day we would see each other for the last time.

ARE YOU AT PEACE WITH YOURSELF AND OTHERS?

THE SEA OF UNLIMITED POSSIBILITIES.

———————I woke up with mixed feelings. Within two hours I would have already been in the car to go back to the airport. I was happy to go home. Anna would certainly listen to me with curiosity when I told her everything I had experienced. Something inside me told me she would understand. That she wouldn‘t find anything "stupid" or "out of this world" in my recount, and this thought reassured me. However, the imminent farewell to Claudio dulled the happiness a bit. He and the trabocco had entered my heart.

With these thoughts, I went to take a shower and then left the room. In the breakfast room today sat an elderly gentleman and a little girl, whom I had never seen before. The gentleman greeted me in a friendly way, and the little girl also nodded before turning back to him, chatting happily. She was wearing a light blue summer dress and had her brown hair tied back in a high ponytail. I assumed the older gentleman was the grandfather. I sat at the empty table next to them.

As I enjoyed a croissant and a cup of coffee, I overheard a few fragments of their conversation. The little girl was saying something to him. At one point her gaze darkened, her smile disappeared and she frowned as if she

were thinking. She also forgot the bread and jam, which her grandfather lovingly reminded her of.
When the little girl suddenly jumped up to take a closer look at a particularly beautiful bird that had just landed outside on the terrace railing, I heard the old gentleman say: “Even little ones have their worries”.
I nodded as they both looked at it. I too had learned something through my grandchildren. “What advice would you give to a child?” I heard him add.
I looked at him. “What do you mean?”, I asked.
“If you had only one sentence at his disposal, what would you share from your life experience with a child who is still at the beginning of their life journey?“
I wanted to say something intelligent, but I couldn‘t find any good answers inside me. I didn‘t see my granddaughters often and there were no other children in my daily life. I had therefore never before found myself in the embarrassing position of having to give advice to a child.
At that moment, the little girl came back and pulled her grandfather by the arm. She wanted to go to the beach. The old gentleman got up, we said goodbye and the two went out, hand in hand. I watched them go.
Rosa Maria came to my table and asked me if I needed anything else. I answered no. When she turned around again, something occurred to me: “Could you prepare some sandwiches for Claudio too, please? I‘ll stop by to

see him before leaving."
Rosa Maria smiled. "Sure with pleasure. I'll get them to you them in a moment."
As I walked to the trabocco, fifteen minutes later, the view seemed startlingly clear.
That day the jetty pointed sharply into the sea. The nets and ropes were clearly distinguishable. The landscape was picturesque like a postcard, without being kitschy. The sea was rough, the waves rose, lapping the sides of the pier and fell again. "The waves really do have an easy time", I thought. "Even if... when there's a storm... they have a lot to do too". I smiled at my own thoughts. Suddenly I froze. Where the hell did all those trabocchi suddenly come from? Was it thanks to the visibility of that day? Claudio had told me that there were many along that stretch of coast, at least two dozen in this area alone, but I had never noticed them before. I saw several that day. One after the other they lined up along the coast, a few hundred meters apart. I noticed that you could look very far that day.
I wondered if there was a Claudio in each trabocco. Were there so many fishermen who did not dare to go out to sea?
"Good morning!", I heard his familiar voice say. Claudio was coming straight towards me. I found it unusual to meet him on the bank, outside the trabocco. He, the jetty, the hut, had been a kind of monad for me in the

last few days.
He smiled: “Nice to see you again”.
We met in front of the blackboard where I had stopped the first day. Many more questions had been added to the first one I had read on my first day.
I looked at Claudio. “Thank you for everything,” I said. It seemed too little, but I lacked the words to do more. How do you describe the feeling of having learned something fundamental? To have cracked that invisible eggshell that surrounded you, and to have finally opened your gaze to the outside world? That something had changed, even if you were not yet clear what that was? How can one express one‘s gratitude for this? Should I have brought him anything?
Claudio shook his head as if he knew exactly what was going through my mind at that moment. “I have you to thank,” he said softly. “I learned a lot from you”.
Now I was even more speechless.
“Through our conversations I was able to retrace my life once again,” he continued, smiling. “This is very valuable to me. Thank you”.
We watched the water in silence for a while.
“Go to sea!” said Claudio suddenly.
There‘s no more time, I meant to say. I have to go to the car immediately, my plane leaves in a few hours. I was about to say this when he said: “I had so many opportunities and I didn‘t take them, because I thought I didn‘t

have time. Now I would have time, but I can't".
I thought about his wife and her health.
"If I could travel today, I would change many things", said Claudio. "I've been to many cities around the world: New York, Barcelona, Tokyo... But I only realised here, at the trabocco, that I've never really been there. I was there, yet I wasn't there."
It seemed to me that I understood what he meant to say.
"You know, it's not a big deal to get on a plane and sleep in a hotel in a foreign city," he continued. "But to truly know and understand a place, its people and their mentality, and what this might mean for your own life - that takes courage. Leaving everything behind and venturing into a new way of life also takes courage. You have the chance to choose. You can still go out and make your dreams come true."
Jokingly, he gave me a soft punch on my side, as if he didn't want to make our last moment so serious. I smiled, keeping my gaze on the horizon. From where I was standing, it seemed that to reach it I just had to walk to the end of pier and keep going. I wondered what I would find at the other end of the sea. Only after a while did I look at Claudio. "I'm glad we met." I tried to swallow the lump that had formed in my throat.
Claudio spread his arms: "Come on!". He hugged me tightly and warmly, like a good friend hugs, and he patted me on the back: "Take care of yourself", he said."

"And put to good use what the trabocco has given you". With these words he turned away and walked along the pier without looking back. I watched him walk until he disappeared into the hut. As I turned to leave, my eyes fell on the blackboard in front of which we‘d been standing all this time.

I read:

WHAT IS THE MOST IMPRESSIVE THING YOU TAKE AWAY FROM THIS JOURNEY?

THE JOURNEY TOWARDS A NEW LIFE

__________There are many different ways to travel. On some trips we just have fun, relax, meet nice people and go home. Nothing more and nothing less. On others, apparently the same thing happens, but in addition we are taken to a place deep within us that we have never explored before.

And this can happen through a brief meeting with a person who asks us with questions we have never asked ourselves. I used to be a person who had traveled the first way. It was only through my journey to the trabocchi that I found out that there is another way. That trip had changed my life, but I didn't know it at first. Usually, we understand the meaning of things only when we look at them in the rear view mirror.

Why do we decide to go to a place? Why had I gone right to the trabocchi? Was it a recommendation from a friend? An ad on the internet? I can no longer recollect. That place had magically attracted me. That's all I know.

My actual journey began with an unspectacular step: a literal step on the jetty close to the sea. Sometimes I wonder what would have happened if I hadn't taken that first step. If I kept walking. Would my vacation have been different? Would I still be the same today? I do not know.

I'm glad everything turned out exactly the way it did. I'm not a believer in fate or astral coincidences but, honestly, what I lived sometimes it makes me think about it.
I've also asked myself if everything is still there now as it was. If I went back to the trabocchi, would I still find everything as the last time I saw it? The sea, the pier, Claudio, Rosa Maria and everyone I met?
Maybe I will go again. Maybe I will not. Much more important than the answer to this question is that I learned on the trabocco that every encounter with people is something special and touches us if we allow it. Many of us are so incredibly busy and overlook things that are important and that really matter. Everything and everyone is important. Everything and everyone is precious. We decide what to make of each moment, who we want to be for ourselves and for others, and whether we will one day venture out to sea.

PATHS EMERGE AS WE TAKE STEPS FORWARD

ABOUT THE AUTHORS

____________Loredana Meduri & Alessandro Spanu are ambassadors of the Dolce Vita.

They have made it their mission to guide people on their journey to happiness by bringing lightness and joy into life and everything they do. As systemic coaches and Dolce Vita experts, they leverage the inspiring way of life in Italy to ignite the spark of joy in workshops, seminars, and personal coaching.

They have captured their extensive knowledge and experiences in books to spread their message of joy and conscious enjoyment. Loredana and Alessandro are dedicated to empowering, encouraging, and inspiring people to live a more serene life.

COACHING THAT ENRICHES LIFE

__________Have you ever thought about what it would be like to increase your quality of life and make the most out of every day? Sometimes, it can be helpful to take time for personal growth.

Coaching can be a valuable opportunity to gain clarity, set goals, and enrich your path. Whether you're seeking professional success or personal fulfillment, together we can find ways to bring about positive changes in your life.

If you're curious about how coaching can positively impact your life, we warmly invite you to explore this possibility. Together, we can work towards ensuring that your life doesn't just exist but flourishes in every moment.

Printed in Great Britain
by Amazon

56517674R00078